GW00696783

I Will Plant Me a Tree

Quoth the good Sir John Gresham of Norfolk fame,
  'I will plant me a tree, my boys;'
So he planted our School that has lived and grown,
  And is growing today, my boys.

Chorus: -   Dig about the roots, my boys,
                See to sun and air, my boys,
                Catch the dew of heaven, my boys,
                Plant your tree to grow.

From an Arbor Day song by Canon A.E. Humphreys,
Governor of the School, and set to music
by Mr G.T. Shaw in 1904.

I Will Plant Me a Tree

An Illustrated History of Gresham's School

Steve Benson

with a chapter on the early years by

Martin Crossley Evans

This book is for the whole family of
Gresham's past, present and future.
It is dedicated to those Greshamians
who gave their lives in two World Wars
and whose names appear
at the end of this history.

Acknowledgements

Many OGs wrote with memories of staff and events. Others sent anecdotes and illustrations.
To all these I am greatly indebted as I am to those whose words, reproduced in the OG
Newsletter or elsewhere, I have used, and attributed, in the text. In particular I am grateful to
Laurence Le Quesne and the late Brian Simon with whom I enjoyed lengthy correspondence.
Former colleagues and Governors have also allowed me hours of their time in valuable dis-
cussions.

The Librarians and Archivists of Uppingham, Clifton, Giggleswick, Rossall and Dover have
been most helpful and informative. Elaine Waterson, the Headmaster's Secretary, and Frances
Chenevix-Trench gave considerable help in the early months and Venetia Davies has willingly
and skilfully undertaken most of the work in preparing the text for the printers. Much assistance and information has been given also by present members of the Gresham's staff, especially John Rayner, as well as the Headmaster, John Arkell. Finally I should like to thank the
Governors who commissioned this History, for allowing me free access to all their records
and minute books, and The Fishmongers' Company, and especially the Clerk Keith Waters
and Archivist Raya McGeorge, for their hospitality and support during my visits to the Hall.

Dr Tony Leech has spent countless hours taking and reproducing photographic illustrations.
Many individuals, notably Jonah Mitchell, have provided other photographs and Dick Bagnall-
Oakeley's extensive photographic archive has been put at our disposal by his son Jeremy. I
am most grateful to them all.

Martin Crossley Evans's acknowledgements for his researches into the first 350 years of the
School's history follow his chapter 'The Early Years' towards the end of this book.

Picture Acknowledgements

Alpine Club 158 (Tom Bourdillon); Camera Press 158 (Peter Brook); Hulton Getty 157 (Tom
Wintringham, Erskine H. Childers); National Portrait Gallery 44 and 157 (Benjamin Britten,
Stephen Spender).

First published 2002
© Gresham's School 2002

ISBN 0-907383-92-0

Project Editor: Susie McSkimming
Designer: Vimbai Shire

Printed and bound by Butler & Tanner Ltd, Frome

Published by James & James (Publishers) Ltd
Gordon House Business Centre
6 Lissenden Gardens
London NW5 1LX

Foreword

Steve Benson is the ideal person to evaluate the pioneering work of Gresham's under Howson and Eccles and of its subsequent development. He has the trained historian's eye for the important issues and the telling details. Thoroughly readable, he often owes his information to reminiscences over a glass of beer rather than to bare statistics. The result is consequently closer to the truth, if occasionally anecdotal, bordering on the legendary. Steve has had close views of Gresham's from most angles: as an assistant master, House Tutor and a Housemaster.

A sensitive musician with a lovely chocolate voice, a memorable play producer, a fine games player, a redoubtable disciplinarian, in the years when everyone forgot how to say boo to a goose, he looked like a beetle-browed buffalo, and he could be frightening. Most of his pupils, however, came to see through the bluster and to value the warm, even soft heart within. If Gresham's has one quality which has survived the century since Howson's arrival, it is its ability to attract staff of that kind: of such varied interests, and so eager to share them with the young, that they could not fail to spark a response. They provided such width of opportunity that the most disparate talents have been able to flourish. That was part of the sunshine which Howson bequeathed to the school, together with the conviction that within the humblest pupil there lurked, perhaps not an Einstein, but a unique contributor to society.

The chapter by Martin Crossley Evans on the earlier years is vital. His painstaking research and scholarship has brought to light much new and fascinating information, without which this book would lack an important dimension.

Finally, we all owe a tremendous debt of gratitude to the Governors and to the Fishmongers' Company for their generosity, encouragement and tolerance – for which we never expressed enough appreciation at the time. Thank you too to the many others who made the job a real, if somewhat hazardous delight, including the many open and responsive boys and girls, whose happiness and success was and always will be our ultimate aim.

Logie Bruce Lockhart
Headmaster 1955–1982

Contents

Preface

This is the first time a History of Gresham's has been undertaken. It is certainly not definitive. Many will look for a mention and be disappointed, others will disagree with conclusions drawn. Any omissions or errors are entirely mine.

In the year of the School's quatercentenary (1955), a 'History and Register' was published. The Revd C.L.S. Linnell wrote a Preface which gave an interesting outline of the Gresham's story. A.B. Douglas produced a masterly register with valuable appendices. Without this excellent reference section, the production of this book would have been far less accurate and far more difficult. Douglas himself owed much to an earlier register of the years 1900–1920 compiled by H.W. Partridge. Otherwise, and apart from a few pamphlets written by J.R. Eccles, a short biography of Howson by J.H. Simpson, and an account of the Newquay years *Gresham's in Wartime* by Philip Newell and Bernard Sankey, much reliance has been placed on *The Gresham*, a remarkable record of the School over the past hundred years especially in the crucial period of Howson's and Eccles' Headships. The *Old Greshamian Newsletter*, notably over the past decade, has been another valuable source through obituaries, reminiscences and correspondence.

As this history concentrates on the last 100 years, from the appointment of G.W.S. Howson and the refounding of the School on its present site along the Cromer Road, it was decided to place the chapter on 'The Early Years' at the end of the book. My friend and former colleague Martin Crossley Evans has researched this period for more than twenty years, revealing many facts and insights previously unrecorded. His section has been written heroically under severe constraints. His meticulous work could have filled a volume twice the size of this.

Sue Smart's touching and recently published story of Gresham's during the First World War, *When Heroes Die*, provides additional information on this traumatic period in the School's history.

Steve Benson
March 2002

Eric Johnson and Geoffrey Gwyther: new boys 1903.

1

The Refounding:

G.W.S. Howson 1900–1919

As early as May 1894 Mr Warden Travers had drawn the attention of the Court of Assistants at Fishmongers' Hall to an urgent financial matter. Numbers 14 to 18 Finsbury Pavement in London formed part of Sir John Gresham's endowment and an eighty-year lease would come to an end at Christmas 1899. The lease provided the endowment with an annual rent of £101. It was clear that the new rents would be such that the income would be far in excess of the needs of the Grammar School housed in the Manor House in Holt. The Charity Commissioners would require a new scheme under the Endowed Schools Act.

During the next five years many options were considered. A Royal Commission looking into the curriculum of county Grammar Schools drew attention to the success of the Paston Grammar School in North Walsham. Gresham's could become a similar centre for county education and 'might have a great future before it' – but the Governors were suspicious of any attempt by an outside body to control their school. Some Governors favoured the setting up of a public school like Uppingham or Repton, others a move out of the county altogether suggesting a link with Dover College or the setting up of a school for girls too. Finally it was decided to build a new school at Waterloo Farm along the Cromer Road out of Holt on land which had been obtained by the Governors as a result of the reorganisation of land holding after the Enclosure Act of 1811.

In June 1899 the surveyor for the Fishmongers' Company, Mr Chatfeild Clarke, presented his plans for a new school with Headmaster's House, boarding accommodation for between forty and sixty boys and up to 280 pupils in all. He made clear where future developments could be made. There was ample space for easily accessible playing fields. The architecture was described as 'a free adaptation of the classical with a gothic spirit'. It was a gamble for the total costs of the new buildings would be £40,000 and the total endowment was only £1,650 but Finsbury Pavement came up trumps: the rent of £101 became £4,700 and the total annual endowment £6,600. It would be a long haul to pay back the necessary loan but it could be done.

The decision was made to offer a generous pension to the current Headmaster, the Revd Reginald Jolliffe Roberts. A new Head would be sought, and to enable

Headmaster: G.W.S. Howson in 1900.

Staff 1900: (left to right)
J.G. Woods; J.R. Eccles;
G.W.S. Howson;
R.H. Langford-James;
J.C. Miller.

Wansbeck House 1902: Mr and Mrs J.C. Miller presiding.

The young schoolmaster: Howson at Newton College 1884.

him to appoint his own staff all existing teachers were given notice. Roberts was to hold office until the end of the summer term 1900. Public advertisements attracted 140 applicants of whom 53 were considered and 12 interviewed. Five were invited to final interviews in London where fifteen Governors were present. On 14 May 1900 a vote was taken on the final two candidates. Four were cast for Walter Sargant (later to become Headmaster of Oakham School) and eleven for George William Saul Howson, who was promptly offered the job. Howson had bombarded the Clerk to the Governors, Sir John Wrench Towse, with questions in letters preserved at Fishmongers' Hall. He had made clear his determination to declare his vision of a modern curriculum unshackled by the 'drudgery' of the classics 'for a school carried on on the lines of compromise of the present provincial grammar school promises to fall short of success.'

Howson had been encouraged by the emphasis in the advertisements on the new buildings and facilities which were already planned. His correspondence with Trowse laid the foundations for a thorough, bold and exhaustive campaign. He was at the top end of the age range suggested by the Governors and he clearly saw this job as his great chance. He produced for the Governors twenty-five copies of a small booklet, published and printed locally in Uppingham, which included his letter of application and testimonials from nine supporters including the Warden of Merton and three headmasters as well as several of his colleagues on the Uppingham staff. Amongst his seven referees were the Earl of Dartmouth and the Master of Marlborough College. Howson's scholarship, his part in the recent construction of modern science laboratories, his broad educational range which included a considerable knowledge of French and German, his experiences as tutor in a boarding house, his energy and enthusiasm, are highlighted by his supporters as is the potential contribution which his sisters Rosa and Mary would make to their brother's Headship. This last point, that Howson was a bachelor, concerned him as he felt it might prejudice his candidature. He made it clear to Trowse that his sisters would provide the household management and feminine influence necessary to a Headmaster who would also be a Boarding Housemaster. A former Uppingham colleague, Revd W.C. Compson, who was now Headmaster of Dover College, wrote tellingly of his commitment to his pupils: 'His love of boys and their pursuits and interests in and out of school is only equalled by his ease in dealing with them and maintaining discipline, which he does without severity.'

George Howson came from a line of schoolmasters. His grandfather, the Revd John Howson, became Second Master at Giggleswick School in Yorkshire, retiring aged 75 after forty-four years' service. Howson's father, William, was the Revd John's third son. He attended Sidney Sussex College, Cambridge, though he did not take a degree, and taught in a succession of schools at Horton-in-Ribbersdale, Alston and Penrith. George was born on 8 August 1860 and was sent to the family school. We know little about his career at Giggleswick since there was no school magazine in his time, though he was clearly one of the brightest pupils and won many prizes for history and geography as well as science. In 1879 he was awarded a Postmastership or Scholarship at Merton College, Oxford, graduating in 1883 with First Class Final Honours in Science. He took a position as assistant master at Newton College in South Devon and then, in 1886, was appointed Senior Science Master at Uppingham by the redoubtable Edward Thring, one of the great reforming Headmasters of the nineteenth century. Thring had only months to live and Howson turned up for interview by mistake, a telegram having been wrongly worded. But he was appointed on the spot, and, although the dynamic years of Uppingham's growth were soon replaced by a far less vigorous regime, he clearly absorbed much of the philosophy of the man who gave him his chance.

Fishing Party, Banffshire 1891. Howson (right) with sister Mary and J.G. Woods (2nd from left) who later became Second Master.

An early Speech Day tea on the Woodlands lawn.

The boarders, December 1900: Howson with sisters Rosa (seated) and Mary.

It has to be said that Howson's fourteen years at Uppingham seem to have been low-key if not exactly anonymous. The sciences were certainly not considered major curriculum subjects even at this relatively progressive school. Classics still ruled the roost, reminding us of the fact that at many public schools in the early and middle Victorian period, science teachers were paid less than classicists and in some cases were not even elected members of the Common Room. Although he enjoyed and played a fair game of Fives and had rowed in a College boat at Merton, Howson was not a great supporter or advocate of team games which still dominated the lives of public schoolboys up and down the land. He founded the Photographic Society and organised outings. He supported the Natural History Society and in 1888 gave 'a most interesting account of a lump of chalk, or rather upon chalk generally' to the fifteen members present. Later he reconstituted the Society and under his forceful Presidency it attracted 200 members. He spoke regularly in debates, showing his radical side when opposing a motion approving of the Primrose League whose aims were 'to bring Upper and Lower Classes into closer contact and to teach the working man something about politics.' Howson asked, 'Who were the Upper Classes and what right had they to show others how to think, or how to enjoy themselves?' The motion was carried. He was forthright, too, in his condemnation of Dr Jameson's attempt, in 1896, to seize the Witwatersrand in South Africa when gold was discovered there. This was a brave statement in the context of the time when considerable patriotic and jingoistic sentiments were being expressed. The chamber was full, over a hundred being present. Howson 'expressed his opinion that Jameson had been no braver than a burglar: there was nothing to admire in mere physical bravery divorced from moral principles.' The school magazine records that 'The speaker was here interrupted, and forced to appeal for order.' Nonetheless the motion condemning the raid was carried by a two-to-one majority.

And so to the entry in the school magazine for 1900: 'We are sorry to have lost Mr Howson and Mr Sergeant but we are glad to welcome Mr Brown and Mr Sweating in their places.' Faint praise for fourteen years.

Despite the appreciative comments made by some colleagues in their testimonials supporting his application to Gresham's, there is little doubt that Howson's north-country upbringing fostered a blunt and forthright character which was not always appreciated by the masters and pupils of a large, established public school and he was by no means universally popular. 'The majority,' in the words of J.H. Simpson who wrote a biography of Howson in 1925, 'regarded him indifferently, as a master having no great influence in the councils of the school. The last fact must always come as a surprise to those who knew him only in Holt – that he does not seem [at Uppingham] to have been one of the men who counted.'

Not that the appointment as Headmaster of Gresham's (until then known as the Free Grammar School of Sir John Gresham at Holt) would have been seen as much of a coup in 1900. Fred Jarvis, the only boarder pupil linking with the days before Howson, who was to become Head of School and a Norfolk clergyman, wrote in 1950 of the facilities of the School under 'Bobbie' Roberts, Howson's predecessor. Three teachers, including Roberts, taught together in the big schoolroom in what is now the Old School House. The noise was considerable, partly because one of the ushers, Billy Thorpe, 'had never heard of discipline or self-discipline' and partly because there were usually boys grouped round the masters' desks receiving instructions in Latin, Mathematics, History or the Catechism. Jarvis attests that good grounding was given nonetheless despite antiquated methods and conditions. 'However,' he goes on, 'it must have seemed a depressing picture to the short, stoutish man who stepped into it [the Schoolroom] during school hours one day dressed in frock coat and silk hat, on a visit of inspection, but whose mind probably envisaged the new buildings which were shortly to begin to rise from the ground on the Cromer Road and the new School he was to create out of the remnants of the old.'

School Prefects, October 1900.

Gresham's boys at Weybourne Station 1903.

Howson fishing in the Banffshire Avon 1891.

In September 1900 this 'new school' was barely at the stage of digging the foundations. There were only forty boys including seven boarders. Yet Howson managed to persuade four men to join him on the staff, two of whom, J.R. Eccles and J.C. Miller, were to give their professional lives to the service of the School. Eccles, who was to become Second Master and to follow in his revered chief's footsteps, almost literally, as Headmaster until his retirement in 1935, wrote to his mother in Little Darwen, Lancashire, after a week at Gresham's: 'It is a great place Holt and I am already quite in love with it. I foresee some difficult work ahead but a great opportunity for making something of the place. All one does is engrossing and life is most exhilarating. I am supremely happy. We feel we are going to make the place go. We like Howson immensely.'

Fortunate, then, or perceptive, or both, in his choice of staff (and many who followed after), Howson had other advantages too. To the delight of his audience during the celebrations surrounding the opening of the new school buildings in October 1903, he gave full expression to these: 'Excellent buildings, laboratories that must be the envy of other schools, air like champagne, and finally a Board of Governors, nine colleagues, and a hundred boys that I would not exchange with any other Headmaster.' Communications had become less tortuous with the coming of the railway to Holt in the 1880s even if the journey to London took more than four hours. And there was the natural situation of the School. North Norfolk hardly fits Noel Coward's famous epithet. It is not flat: in fact it has a ridge, the Cromer Ridge, and a bump, the Beeston Bump. There are woodlands, heathlands, salt marshes, beaches, rich farmland and huge skies. The climate is bracing and the whole coastline bristled, in those days, with sanatoria for the unfortunates who suffered from consumption. It was a healthy place for the young, and from the start Howson encouraged his boys to get out on Sundays on foot or on bicycles to discover the glories of the Norfolk countryside and coastline. Then he had the enormous opportunities afforded a pioneer Headmaster. Generous funds were there to build a brand new school. In the ensuing years many Governors and

Heads travelled to Holt to view the boarding accommodation, the laboratories, the classrooms. Howson also enjoyed the energetic support of his Governors, led by the Fishmongers' Company and the man who was to be Chairman throughout his Headship, Sir Edward Busk, an enthusiastic educationalist who became Vice-Chancellor of London University.

A study from the 1903 prospectus.

If the omens were propitious, clarity of vision, organisation and leadership were still needed. These were supplied in full measure by Howson. The curriculum was to be modern. When W.F. Bushell, who was on the Gresham's staff from 1907 to 1912 and who later became Head of three Headmasters' Conference (HMC) schools, was himself a boy at Charterhouse in the 1890s, only 70 of the 550 pupils were allowed some freedom from the Classics. Howson's view of this had been made clear in his 1902 Prospectus. He quoted a recent speech by Lord Rosebery in his Rectorial Address at Glasgow University: 'The training of our schools and colleges must daily become more and more the training for action . . . for practical purposes. Are there not thousands of lads today plodding away, or supposed to be plodding away, at the ancient classics who will never make anything of these classics, who will cast them into space and never re-open them? Think of the wasted time . . . entirely wasted as far as available knowledge is concerned . . .' Small wonder that the mathematician Bushell was attracted to what was offered at Gresham's. The three 'R's, Geography, History, English, French, Natural Science (including principles applicable to agriculture like land surveying and bookkeeping), Drawing, Music and Drill were compulsory. Older boys learned, in addition, Latin or German, Algebra and Euclid (Geometry). Greek was an optional extra (£1 per term). Howson was a pioneer in designing a curriculum to interest all boys. It was similar to that on offer to the minority modern side pupils in the bigger public

The 1902 Cross Country.

15

Picnic on Blakeney Point, 1901.

schools, but the difference was marked because here it was the norm and not an inferior alternative to the Classics. Many who applied for jobs at Holt were delighted and refreshed by this approach. The Balfour Education Act of 1902 stimulated a move towards science and gave local authorities the duty of founding and financially supporting new (and existing) grammar schools. Howson anticipated the move. He was not concerned with public examinations but he did seek to win Oxbridge scholarships for his brightest pupils. The Honours Boards in Big School bear testimony to his success and that of his successors. In the December examinations at Oxford in 1918, only weeks before Howson's death, no fewer than five Open Scholarships were won – and this from a School (excluding the Preparatory Department) of only 200. And nor was this an isolated case. In 1915, for example, Gresham's boys won two of the three annual and much coveted Balliol History Scholarships. Howson was well aware of the value to the School's reputation of such academic distinction.

Howson's vision encompassed much more than the classroom. Music played a major role in the School's life and he was fortunate to enlist the services of Geoffrey Shaw and later Walter Greatorex as Directors of Music. Weekly recitals by staff and boys became central to the calendar as were periodic orchestral concerts. Music was also essential to the annual Shakespeare play produced in the woods from 1902 onwards which became a major Norfolk event, enhanced by the building of the Open Air Theatre, under the direction of Messrs Spiers and McNeile with boy labour, in 1907. Shaw's incidental music was complemented by

E.A. Robertson's directing skills. Reviews appeared in the national, as well as the local, press. Debates were held regularly from the earliest days, a magnificent pun being perpetrated in a speech by E.M. Brooke-Booth supporting the motion advocating greater protection for wild birds. He preferred the song of birds to their flesh and, as a Norfolk man, could do no more for a county famous for its rooks, than to support their caws. Topical subjects for discussion were chosen and the School's enlightened ethos was well illustrated when a packed house voted by a large majority, in 1909, in favour of the extension of the franchise to women. It took a World War to convince Parliament. Lectures with slides were popular with J.R. Eccles prominent. By the end of his time at Gresham's it would have been unusual indeed for any boy not to have learned much about climbing in the Dolomites. The Natural History Society had many branches covering Botany, Geology, Photography, Zoology and Ornithology leading to half-day expeditions along with their Architectural and Sociological fellows. Again it must be pointed out that such activity in the years before the Great War were, if not unknown at traditional public schools, at least rare. At Gresham's they were part of the educational process.

So, then, the School curriculum and its essential extra-curricular associations were liberal and enlightened. So too was Howson's attitude towards games. Contrary to some accounts, colours were awarded for excellence in team sports and by 1916 the appropriate badges worn on the blazer, but games were never allowed to become predominant. Success was applauded, the School Magazine containing match reports and team 'portraits' at the end of the season, but inter-schools fixtures were not allowed: matches were played against Cambridge Colleges and touring sides and those raised by local worthies. Cheering was forbidden, though clapping was sanctioned. This produced a dissenting letter to *The Gresham* in December 1910: 'May I suggest that the School be allowed to shout

Howson, camera in hand, with a group of boys by the Glaven.

Fives at the Old School House c.1901.

during Football or Hockey matches? There seems to be a lack of interest in matches at present. Clapping, although excellent in the concert or lecture room, is but a poor way of expressing one's emotions on the field.' No action was taken. Boys were to enjoy their sports and to do their best, but there should be no philathleticism which pervaded most other schools, and performance and talent in acting, debating, music, natural history or academia were equally valued. By all accounts, it worked – to the greater good of all and the greater happiness of the unathletic. Small wonder that the name of Gresham's became respected for this unusually healthy and balanced approach to sport. The only inter-school competition allowed and encouraged was in shooting and this became a major success (given much coverage, once again, in *The Gresham*) due to the early foundation of a Cadet Corps in 1902. Annual Camps were a great attraction and on several occasions favourable comments were made officially about the behaviour and bearing of the Gresham's cadets. Howson cannot have been unaware of the value of this to the growing reputation of the School. There is a photograph of the officers of the Aldershot Camp in the summer holidays of 1905 where the salute was taken by Field Marshal Lord Roberts. At the feet of the legendary 'Bobs' sit the Gresham's officers, Captain Miller and Lieutenant Eccles. In 1907 the Officers' Training Corps replaced the Cadets and in that year the Gresham's VIII competed in the Schools of the Empire Shooting Competition, coming second to Brisbane GS in Australia and first in all the Schools in Great Britain. It must have been with particular satisfaction that Howson would have noted that Uppingham came second. The extraordinary performance of so small and 'new' a School was a source of pride but merited less exposure in *The Gresham* than the report of a lecture on Purcell. Such was his insistence on balance that Howson made no mention of this shooting triumph in his Speech Day address which came but a fortnight later. The Chief Guest, the High Sheriff of Norfolk, fortunately had prepared his brief (or had been given one) so honour (and PR) was satisfied.

Swedish Drill.

Probably the best known of Howson's innovations, however, was the 'Honour System' as it came to be known. There were no printed rules at Gresham's. Howson made clear what he wanted and left it to the honour of his boys. He trusted them to carry out his wishes. He believed that an inner discipline was more potent than outward compulsion. He put the responsibility on the boys and in their sense of what was fitting. Moral excellence was to count above all other. Within a week or two of a boy's arrival at Gresham's, he had an interview with the Headmaster. After speaking of his moral ideals for the School, Howson asked the boy to swear three things: not to smoke, not to swear and not to say or do anything indecent. If any of these promises were broken, the boy was to report himself to his Housemaster. If he saw or heard anyone else breaking them he was to persuade that person to own up and, failing that, to report the perpetrator himself. Many have protested that this must have placed an intolerable pressure on young boys. Howson was unwavering. He believed in his 'system' (not that he called it such) and he believed in his boys. J.R. Eccles recounts overhearing a conversation between Howson and another who was excusing a boy for a fault with the expression 'Boys will be boys'. Howson's reply was, 'Why should they not be men?'

Lady Lillian Bull, whose husband was a Conservative MP and a solicitor in the City, visited her 17-year-old son Stephen at Gresham's in October 1921. Howson was dead by this time but he had once stayed with the Bulls at their London home. She observed the Gresham's morality in action, writing in her diary: 'Stephen himself has grown up a great deal lately but is still curiously young and pure in mind and thought. I had six of his friends out to different meals . . .What struck me about them was their modesty and keenness in doing their best for their House and keeping up the high standards of the School. They discussed many social questions and seemed thoroughly alive although simple and free from any "side" or "swank". The memory of their old Head is still very present with them . . . whether it is because games are not thought of more than work or the peaceful

Cadet Corps on parade c.1906.

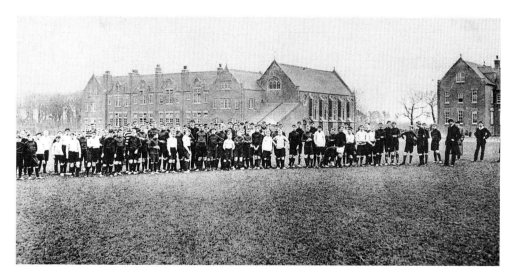

Before the Steeplechase c.1908.

Arbor Day 1904.

surroundings, they certainly strike me as an extremely well behaved, happy-look-ing lot of boys. I think they have a good deal of freedom and are left on their hon-our which seems to work.'

The place of the Housemaster was crucial in creating the unique atmosphere at Gresham's. Both Howson and Eccles, at Uppingham and at Clifton respectively, had come across the green baize door. Both were dedicated to removing it. Prefects at Gresham's were vital as role models and as supporters of the Housemaster's authority but they did not run the House as at so many other schools. The Housemaster walked freely in the corridors of his House and chat-ted to his boys in the dormitories every night. Dinner parties would stop for House Prayers and guests would troop in to attend. Howson introduced Arbor days in 1902. The outstanding boys would each plant a tree in his name on the boundary between the cricket field and the athletics field or nearer to the School House – practical and symbolic acts in the new School grounds. From 1908 their names were placed on a Roll of Honour before such a term obtained a more poignant significance after 1914. Much was expected of them. 'In our Prefects,' said Howson at an early Arbor day, 'we look for unflinching straightforwardness, desperate earnestness, and untarnished honour.' To some the word 'desperate' must have carried a more modern connotation than the Edwardian. But it was to the Housemaster that the boys looked for leadership and guidance. Assistant staff too were encouraged to get to know their pupils. In the early days, of course, num-bers were very small and such things were made easier. But as the School grew, so did the strength of the relationship between staff and boys – and between staff and Head. Howson consulted his staff; where there was disagreement he often took a vote. He demanded loyalty but had the wisdom to see that in order to gain it, he must take an interest in those who worked with him and listen to their opin-ions. He was prepared to delegate. But he set the agenda and he would always say that a small school was essential, which is why he was reluctant to increase numbers above 220. So much depended on his individual knowledge of his boys, his staff and all that went on.

If he was fortunate in his staff, then he should also take credit for appointing

First Arbor Day. Howson with the chosen few plant-ing copper beeches on the playing fields 1902.

Bengal Lodge (later Kenwyn) c. 1906: Gresham's boys in the Cromer Road.

them. Of course some came and went rapidly not least because wages were low. Others, like G.T. Shaw, W.F. Bushell, J.H. Simpson, D.L. Hammick (a fine chemist who was popular because he tobogganed with the boys), stayed for relatively short periods. Hammick left for a brilliant career at Oxford University. Shaw was too fine a musician to be held for long despite his love of Norfolk and he went on to become an outstanding School Inspector. But he sent his three sons to Gresham's. Bushell had to move as his promotion path in Mathematics was blocked by A.H. Spiers. He went as Head of the Modern Side to Rossall and thence to Solihull, Michaelhouse (Natal) and Birkenhead for his three Headships. But he never forgot his debt to Howson and Gresham's: 'No man could have had a better start in his scholastic life. There was a fresh breeze blowing in education. Every member of that distinguished staff would have agreed. Many left the school to work elsewhere in the search for promotion and carried into the world the ideas and ideals they had imbibed.' J.H. Simpson, Howson's biographer, was on the staff for only two years but, again, Gresham's was a revelation and a lifelong inspiration. He returned in 1910 to his old school, Rugby, and at 36 was appointed to found the progressive Rendcomb College in Gloucestershire, financially supported by Noel Wills of tobacco fame. Later Simpson moved on to become Principal of St Mark and St John College, Chelsea, where he had a considerable modernising influence upon the training of teachers. One of Simpson's first appointments at Rendcomb was C.H.C. Osborne, who joined the Gresham's staff in 1913 and was remembered for his refreshingly modern approach to teaching. Another of Howson's most promising early appointments, L.K. Meryon, was lost climbing in the Alps; Vivian Smith, a much admired Art Master, was killed in the trenches.

Howson plus dog outside the Old School House 1900.

Other staff came and stayed. Eccles, Howson's loyal deputy and successor, arrived at the same time as Howson. So did J.C. Miller, founder of the OTC and first Housemaster, in 1911, of Farfield. Still in harness, Miller died in 1928. So too, in the same year, did E.A. Robertson, best remembered for his brilliant

Guard of Honour at the Opening of the New School buildings.

Shakespeare productions in the Open Air Theatre or Theatre-in-the-Woods. Then there were D.A. Wynne-Willson, first Housemaster of the Junior House; the Revd Frank Field, School Chaplain and Housemaster to the Day Boys in Bengal Lodge; C.H. 'Toc' Tyler of the beautiful bass voice; 'Pa' Daniel; 'P' Partridge; the kindly, crippled G.R. Thompson who, according to his former pupil Kemys Bagnall-Oakeley, 'kept wicket without crouching because he didn't need to', and was an excellent Maths teacher; Miss Bristow, whose 'encouragement and open minded-ness' meant so much to her pupils as she pioneered the 'new' Art Department after the Thatched Buildings were opened in 1921; Walter ('Gog') Greatorex, writer of that fine hymn tune 'Woodlands', good friend to many a sensitive youngster like Stephen Spender and the organist whose playing Auden compared favourably with that of Albert Schweitzer; all were appointed by Howson. The longest-serving of them all was Lt. Col. J.H. 'Joe' Foster, the first Housemaster of Howson's, as School House became, who taught French colloquially and by the 'modern method', becoming Second Master and, on his retirement, the only Assistant Master in the history of the School to be made a Governor.

The new buildings were not ready for occupation until 1903 when Field Marshal Sir Evelyn Wood VC, Governor and Fishmonger, inspected a Guard of Honour drawn up outside the Headmaster's house. Fred Jarvis, Head of School at the time, recalls how Howson had taken his three senior boys to camp out in the new build-ings just prior to the official opening. By this time numbers had risen to over a hundred and various arrangements had had to be made to accommodate them. Wansbeck House (between White Lion corner and the Old School House) was adapted, the School House extended to take more boarders and along the Cromer Road, Bengal Lodge (later Kenwyn and then Old Kenwyn) was purchased in 1901 to accommodate day boys. Such was the logjam that, before he took over as Housemaster in the Old School House in 1903, J.R. Eccles had to board his boys at the Weybourne Springs Hotel, journeying back and forth by train four times a day from May to July.

By the time Eccles moved into the newly purchased and extended Woodlands

Official opening of New School buildings 30 September 1903: Howson with Field Marshal Sir Evelyn Wood, VC, and Sir John Wrench Towse, Clerk to the Governors.

in 1905 the numbers were over 150. Before long plans were drawn, again by Chatfeild Clarke, for a third boarding house, Farfield (opened under J.C. Miller in 1911), by which time the Old School House had become the Junior House run by D.A. Wynne-Willson. When the First World War broke out, numbers had risen to 230. The nature of the School had changed greatly. The majority of boys were now boarders, coming from all over England (and including at least one lofty and unhappy Scot, John Reith). There were those who did not appreciate the way that Gresham's was evolving into a public school without that distinctive Norfolk flavour which they perceived to be the intention of its first Founder, the good Sir John. Its second Founder, George Howson, had his uneasy moments too. J.H. Simpson recalls that Howson was far from convinced of the merits of public schools. He could be scathing in his comments about them. Not that he wanted his School to remain a parochial Grammar School but he had concerns about the snobbishness and class consciousness of public schools and their parental patrons. However, he was elected a member of Headmasters' Conference (founded by Thring in 1869) in 1906 and so far overcame his scruples that he was co-opted onto its committee in 1914, 1917 and 1918, becoming Chairman of the Public School Hymn Book Sub-Committee and a member of the Sub-Committee on Infectious Illness. Thus far at least he became a member of the Establishment. The scheme under which the School was administered, accepted by the Charity Commissioners and approved 'by Her Majesty, in Council' in October 1899, spelt out the practical application of the principles laid down by Sir John Gresham in 1555. Four Holt Scholarships were to be awarded each year to pupils resident within five miles of the School with free tuition provided. Four County Scholarships were also awarded each year to boys whose parents or guardians were resident in Norfolk, providing free tuition and a substantial grant towards boarding expenses. The cost to the Governors of these forty places was considerable and ensured a strong local flavour to the School although the increasing number of fee-paying distance boarders clearly broadened and diluted the mixture.

Classroom in the New School building.

Laboratories in the New School building.

23

Above and below: *Laying of the Chapel Foundation stone, June 8th 1912, by Sir Edward Busk, Chairman of Governors.*

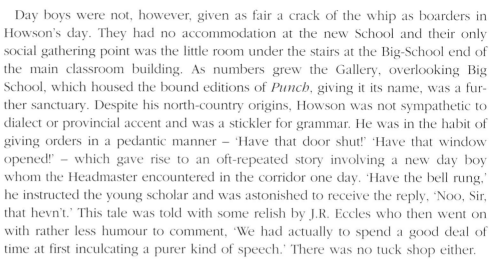

Day boys were not, however, given as fair a crack of the whip as boarders in Howson's day. They had no accommodation at the new School and their only social gathering point was the little room under the stairs at the Big-School end of the main classroom building. As numbers grew the Gallery, overlooking Big School, which housed the bound editions of *Punch*, giving it its name, was a further sanctuary. Despite his north-country origins, Howson was not sympathetic to dialect or provincial accent and was a stickler for grammar. He was in the habit of giving orders in a pedantic manner – 'Have that door shut!' 'Have that window opened!' – which gave rise to an oft-repeated story involving a new day boy whom the Headmaster encountered in the corridor one day. 'Have the bell rung,' he instructed the young scholar and was astonished to receive the reply, 'Noo, Sir, that hevn't.' This tale was told with some relish by J.R. Eccles who then went on with rather less humour to comment, 'We had actually to spend a good deal of time at first inculcating a purer kind of speech.' There was no tuck shop either.

Apart from the new houses, there was only one other major construction during Howson's Headmastership. From the early days he had advocated the building of a Chapel to be the focal point of the School day and the heart of the School's ethos. In 1912 an appeal was launched using the ingenious pretext of the 350th anniversary of the actual opening of the School in 1562. Finances were tight and the foundation stone remained a lonely pedestal for a time before building began, but on 23rd January 1916 Howson himself symbolically turned the key in the door before the assembled pupils, staff and clergy. The former pupils were, of course, otherwise engaged.

The shadow of the First World War hung over Holt from September 1914. Clive Rouse was one of many who had a brother at the front and well remembered the regular announcement of casualties by the Headmaster in Big School. He recalled a pretty austere life with, at first, fears of amphibious landings at Weybourne. Kemys Bagnall-Oakeley remembered, as a youngster in the Old School House, sleeping with an evacuation pack under his pillow. In lighter vein he recounted the occasion when all boys rose in the middle of the night and began a practice withdrawal down the Norwich Road. Government instructions stated that 'all livestock should be released and driven ahead' to make life difficult for the advancing enemy. The boys of the Junior House dutifully released Wynne-Willson's pigs. Punishment did not follow but the boys were tasked with rounding up the animals in the morning with little success until a leader emerged, one John Daly, later to become a Bishop. Bagnall-Oakeley also recalled returning from lessons alone and in pitch darkness one evening. He was passing through the Churchyard when suddenly an unearthly shattering roar erupted immediately overhead. It was not the wrath of God but a low-flying Zeppelin starting up its engines before moving off on a bombing raid, having glided in over the Norfolk coast to avoid the attentions of anti-aircraft batteries.

The Gresham became, like so many other school magazines during the First World War, a catalogue of sad little obituaries and tributes from brother officers and commanders to comfort parents, sweethearts and wives. Rosa and Mary

Howson, spinster sisters of their brother and housekeeper and matron respectively in the Headmaster's House, did much to keep in touch with former pupils at the front and to keep up to date the list of past members of the School serving in His Majesty's forces. Their efforts and the additional researches of Mr Eccles produced details of just over 500 of whom 100 were killed or died on active service – 20 per cent of those who enlisted or were called up. Many old boys came back on leave before returning to their units and often to their deaths. The strain and the pain Howson must have suffered surely contributed to the undermining of his health. In 1917 he was taken ill and was away from his desk (though not from decision making) for several months. There are indications that he suffered increasingly from diabetes in an age before insulin. He never regained his full strength but he worked on. In July 1918 he made a noticeably brief report to parents, staff, pupils and Governors at Speech Day when certificates rather than prizes were awarded because 'they should be perceived as luxuries at a time when economy should be practised.' He congratulated the School Corps, he commended especially the work of the Natural History Society, he applauded the five pupils who had gained open awards at Oxford and Cambridge and a sixth at the Imperial College of Science. And he announced the formation of a War Memorial Committee to raise funds to complete the stalls, panelling and screen in the Chapel. Then came the Armistice and his address in Chapel the day after. It was concise and uncompromising as ever. 'We have to make a new world, worthy of the lives which have been given to bring us to this day of opportunity.'

The Chapel nearing completion.

And then he was gone. He went up to London in the New Year to attend the Headmasters' Conference and also a meeting of the War Memorial Committee but on arrival was too ill to attend either. He returned to Holt at his own urgent request arriving on Sunday 5 January. The following Tuesday he died and was buried close to the School Chapel. His doctor's certificate gave the causes of death as 'chronic nephritis and degeneration of the cardiac muscle leading to heart failure'. He was 58 years old.

What do we know of Howson the man? There are two scrapbooks of photographs mainly from the 1890s. Possibly the earliest shows Howson in gown and mortar-board with a group of boys. Underneath is scrawled in pencil 'Newton Abbey'. It appears to have been taken during his time teaching in Devon between 1883 and 1886 and depicts a slim man with half a smile and a smudge of a moustache. The boys are posed in light-hearted fashion, one reading a magazine. There is a touch of pastiche here; Howson could not have taken himself too seriously at this stage. Another shows the 'Giggleswick School Entrance' in wintertime, snow on the ground and two boys perched gargoyle-like on the pillars guarding the door. Howson probably took this photograph himself as he did many others showing groups of family and friends at, presumably, country-house parties (tennis racquets to the fore) or on walks or picnics. He appears in a number of others, clean-shaven in the 1890s, a teacher at Uppingham on holiday in Banffshire with his sister Mary and friends (one of whom, Sholto Johnstone-Douglas, was later to paint his portrait which hangs in Big School). Several of the party carry fishing rods.

Part of the Gresham family motto 'Fiat Voluntas Tua' on the Chapel door.

Howson (front centre) with Speech Day audience in the Theatre-in-the-Woods 1908.

Howson himself is snapped in the middle of the Scottish Avon, up to his thighs in his waterproofs. He was clearly an ardent fisherman and J.H. Simpson remarks that 'he had a wide knowledge of the wet-fly streams of the north.' Simpson was present later on, after 1910, when Howson would gather a party once or twice a year at Bolton Abbey, Wharfedale. It was a kind of 'home life' for him and it was on these carefree holidays that Simpson noted: 'He showed an infectious buoyancy and gaiety of spirit that I only suspected to exist.' He travelled abroad, according to his albums, in Italy, France (Chartres 1895) and Austria. When he moved from Uppingham to Gresham's in 1900, he recruited former colleagues from Newton College, A.H. Spiers and J.J. Cross. He inspired loyalty as well as friendship. And he repaid it with generosity.

Much is written about the warmth of his welcome and hospitality at Holt. In his own living room he relaxed and shone. Parents, guests and Old Boys were always received with courtesy and kindness. Geoffrey Shaw recalled, 'An evening in his company was a refreshment. Shrewd and humorous, with a fund of good stories and apt illustrations at his command, he excelled in fireside conversation . . . and who will ever forget the charm of his after-dinner speeches . . .' One of his first Heads of School, C.H. Fitch, recalled, 'He was above and beyond all a character builder and maker of traditions. We who had the inestimable privilege of being with him in those early years felt this purpose thrilling through his every word and action.' Fred Jarvis, who later joined Simpson on the holiday parties at Bolton Abbey, on the Broads and on the Thames, said that he was speaking for many Old Boys in saying, 'We think of him as one who has been to us a very good father; who gave us our best gifts, our highest ideals.'

As has been mentioned already, he consulted with his staff and excited them with the breadth and conviction of his vision in building a new kind of school based on trust and individual commitment. His manner was quietly decisive, his keen glance betokening unusual power and discernment. He showed serenity under pressure and was unruffled. A former colleague from Uppingham, visiting Holt for the first time after the move to the new buildings, confessed himself amazed at the strength and dominance of a man who had been of so little influence and importance at his former school. However, both Simpson and W.F. Bushell noted that as a Headmaster he was not exactly popular. Many, even J.R. Eccles, confessed to being uneasy in his presence. And young masters were genuinely fearful of not being capable of living up to the very high standards he demanded.

His appearance, as the years passed, thickened, becoming heavy, almost clumsy, his complexion florid, his manner of speaking abrupt. Some felt that he was prone to passing moral judgement, that they were being 'got at', that his humour was rather one-sided. Some labelled him 'disingenuous'. There is no doubt that to small boys (as to grown men) he could be frightening, sarcastic and quite threatening. In later years he reduced a group of new boys, sent up from the Junior House to meet him, to stuttering incoherence by apparently losing his temper because one of them failed to use the word 'Sir' in a quivering response. Francis King, aged 8, son of the Rector of Holt and thrilled to be riding in an open carriage to Norwich with this great man and his sisters, was torn off a strip after replying pleasantly to a question from Rosa Howson for 'not removing his cap and standing up when addressing a lady' – though quite whether such a thing was reasonable in the travelling circumstances is another matter. King describes Howson's progress through the main classroom building towards the end of the First World War: 'To me he seemed Napoleonic as he paced down the corridor, short, and putting on weight, his hands clutching his gown, nose in the air: he scarcely deigned

The Johnson brothers (1903-1918). Eric, the eldest, claimed to be 'the first boy into Woodlands' in 1905 – through a window as Eccles had mislaid the key.

Shooting VIII 1906. Captain Miller (centre) with Sgt Steer behind him. Cadet John (later Lord) Reith seated extreme right.

a glance as we respectfully drew aside.' G.E. Hutchinson, like King at School during the final years of Howson's Headship, refers to the one recorded occasion when a public caning was carried out of three boys caught out at night and smoking – it was a source of pride and one of the central planks of Howson's system that windows were not barred, as at so many schools, and doors were not locked at 'lock-up'. On this occasion Hutchinson recalls the impression of immense authority which permeated Big School. Apart from this event, he remembers 'no punishment except moral obloquy!' He also stated that 'on the whole we were more humanely treated than were the boys in practically every other public school in Britain.' However, Howson imprinted the Uppingham custom of insisting that only School Prefects be allowed to wear trousers with pockets. Whether this was to improve manners and discourage slouching, to teach stoicism in the east winds of winter, or whether Howson was keen to remove baser temptations from his innocent flock is not clear. Returning for a moment to corporal punishment, Howson alone administered it, sparingly, although there is one suggestion, and only one, that he did allow Prefects to beat with permission. Francis King recalls that the one occasion when he ever heard a member of staff swear was when 'Pa' Daniel used the word 'damnable' in his hearing in connection with a Prefect beating that had 'gone too far'. There is very little reference to beating in any memoir and it is only fair to repeat Hutchinson's reference to the 'humane' treatment of Gresham's boys. Eccles put a stop to beating altogether.

Much can be learned about Howson as Headmaster from his Speech Day addresses which became progressively more concise as the years passed – though in inverse proportion to the length of those given by the man whose vision, staunch support and strong leadership as Chairman of Governors was so crucial to Howson's success, Sir Edward Busk. Both were forthright speakers but it is important to note Howson's wit and humour especially before 1914. It is also from his recorded speeches that we learn something of the man from his own mouth for, apart from a few sermons, his words were never published. Few letters are extant and he wrote no autobiography or memoir. In 1910 he showed at least that he was aware of the criticism levelled at his 'honour system' by outsiders: 'I have been told, twice, that Gresham's School manufactures prigs. I was not disturbed by this unhappily expressed statement for I felt that this would-be detractor told me clearly that the boys of this school have high standards and are not afraid to live up to them . . . There are many still who think that boys cannot reach a reasonably high standard of life. I am glad to think that they can, and do.' And in 1912 he summarised his aims and his priorities: 'There is something more important than the [academic] work of a School. We recognised from the start that the vital question was not what the boys learn but what they are. Our foundation stone was trust. We declined to build an altar to the God of athletics preferring him as a servant . . . and the results? I like to think they are indicated in the faces of those standing around you and by the reputation of the Old Boys . . . It would be absurd for us to claim originality of purpose in what has been done. What we realise is that we are singularly fortunate in our opportunity and in the responsive

Writing to the boys at the front: postcard from Rosa Howson to Private Claude Rouse.

Photography in the School woods: Howson in mortar board.

Staff, 1908.

help we have received from our boys, more especially from the hand of pioneers who laid the traditions, and I can say, and I do now, with gratitude, "They were well and truly laid!"'

His death was sudden and, despite his long illness and absence, unexpected. Sir William Bull MP, whose son Stephen had recently arrived at Gresham's and whose younger son Anthony was to enter the school a few years later, wrote in his diary on 12 January 1919, 'I only learned by accident yesterday that Howson, the head-master at Gresham's School at Holt had died on Friday last. It is almost a National Disaster because I think Howson was a kind of new and more broadminded and enlightened Arnold and was making a determined effort to get schools out of the ruck into which they have fallen. Although I knew him slightly, I feel a great per-sonal loss.' Howson had, in fact, stayed with the Bulls in London soon after their eldest son entered Gresham's, in December 1917. His 'thank you' letter is full of humanity and humour. He describes his ingenuity whilst boarding a rush-hour train, 'stealing a barrow' when he failed to find help from 'porters proud as Lucifer with an air of "engaged 'til February"' and how he carried out a 'flanking move-ment and brazenly wheeled my truck onto Platform 9.' He went on: 'I enjoyed my visit and greatly appreciated the cordial welcome I found. I tried hard not to be jealous of Sir William and you but there comes an ache for children of one's own.' It is hard to read these words merely as the ploy of a consummate public-relations practitioner who knows he has hooked some influential parents. They reveal, too, the essential loneliness of the dedicated bachelor.

The Gresham for 1 March 1919 is devoted to Howson's memory: the bare facts of his death, the description of his burial, the coffin covered with the School flag, the simple ceremony and the committal 'on the south side of the Chapel, half-way between the south porch and the vestry door. No other spot would have done.' And then came the Memorial Service, J.R. Eccles' address to the School and the tributes from Eccles himself, former staff, former pupils and friends. The local press gave coverage, of course, but significantly so did *The Times* and *The Times Educational Supplement*. Dr Theodore Ackland, for twenty years a Governor and parent of a former pupil, wrote in *The Times* of 10 January of Howson's personal influence over the boys and of 'the high tone that prevailed throughout the School', the courtesy and the friendliness. The emphasis on personal development over admitted academic success was a fair judgement and brought Howson public recognition. It was W.F. Bushell, however, who paid his old chief the greatest compliment in *The Times Educational Supplement* on 14 August. Under the title 'A Great Headmaster' his article covered the whole front page and half the second. Eccles expressed the belief that this article was one of the main reasons why Howson's work at Holt became so well known among educationalists. Bushell ranged over the whole remarkable period. Because Howson had refused to be hidebound by public examinations (Scholarship work being always excepted) he allowed his colleagues and his pupils a freer hand. 'Intellectual freedom' is how Bushell described it and this continuing aspect of teaching at Gresham's was warmly commended later on by arguably Gresham's greatest scientist Professor Sir Alan Hodgkin, Nobel Prize Winner, President of the Royal Society and sometime Master of Trinity College, Cambridge. Art exhibitions, music and the pastoral plays in the Open Air Theatre were all part of 'a real liberality' in education. Bushell then described the burning desire for the best which permeated the whole place and the importance of sport as a 'recreation rather than a cult.' And then came his masterly explanation of the honour system and arguments in its favour countering the various charges against it. He went on to commend Howson's handling of his staff which 'brought out all that is best in a man.' He gave a glimpse of Howson the aesthete in stating that in School House, antique furniture, prints, pictures and fittings belonging to the Headmaster overflowed into the boys' corridors, studies and dining hall with civilising effect. The grounds and the buildings were immaculately kept and boys, staff and parents could take a real pride in their surroundings. In terms of discipline Howson preferred 'the internal discipline based on the goodwill of the boys' to 'the external discipline of fear.' Courtesy, good manners, punctuality, friendliness were the 'outward signs of the inward life.' Howson's insistence on keeping the numbers below 250, when he could clearly have taken more had he wanted, revealed his insistence on the importance of his own influence over all the boys and staff if his system based on personal relationships and individual trust was to succeed. In this he was at one with the other great modernising Headmasters of his time, Percival of Clifton, Almond of Loretto, Sanderson of Oundle and, of course, Thring of Uppingham. Bushell ended with these words: 'The world outside may have known little of him. From those who knew him came the reverent affection due to genius. That is his reward. He would not ask for more.'

Possibly because he died in harness, possibly because he had no urge to do so,

Boys congregate at the first sanatorium (now part of Oakeley House).

*The last photograph:
Howson and his prefects
July 1918.*

Howson never wrote about the influences which formed his educational philoso-phy. Thring, of course, he knew and Sanderson of Oundle was a contemporary; both were, like Howson, pioneers in the Arnold tradition. There are glimpses of more. A photograph in his private album of children in Shakespearean costume is annotated in his hand, 'Abbotsholme 1894'. And Abbotsholme was, with Bedales, one of the first progressive schools founded in the 1890s. Did Howson spend time with Abbotsholme's founder Dr Cecil Reddie? In 1900 just before he became Headmaster, Howson visited at least three times in his rooms at Whitehall one of the great educationalists of the age, the young and dynamic Michael Sadler who was engaged in writing eleven volumes of reports on all aspects of secondary edu-cation in England, comparing it with the educational systems in Europe, America and India. In the years leading up to Balfour's 1902 Education Act, Sadler was in constant demand as speaker and writer of articles for newspapers and journals. Howson used a quotation from Sadler's writings in his first School Prospectus in 1900: 'There seems like a great need in England of first-class secondary schools giving a purely modern education of the highest quality, based chiefly on linguis-tic discipline in English, French and German, going to a high point in Mathematics, teaching History, Geography and Literature searchingly, and disciplining every boy in natural sciences – such a type of liberal education being a natural avenue to intellectual interest in modern commerce and industry.' He had quoted these words in his letter of application to the Governors. They knew the man they were employ-ing. It was a brave decision on their part but Howson had not prevaricated.

Howson's approach was practical, even pragmatic. There was very little of the crankiness which underlies the true progressive or revolutionary. However, and probably on the prompting of his disciple, J.H. Simpson, he did invite, at short notice, the American psychotherapist Homer Lane to give a lecture to the boys at

32

Gresham's on his groundbreaking 'Junior Republics' in America. Lane had been invited to set up an experimental school for delinquents in Dorset, to be called the 'Little Commonwealth', and was on a speaking visit to Norfolk in 1913. Quite what the docile pupils of Gresham's made of it all – especially when informed that Mr Lane had been sentenced by a pupils' court to a period of wood-sawing for some perceived misdemeanour – is not recorded. Open to new ideas he may have been but Howson was hardly a radical extremist. Simpson records that during one of his many spirited discussions on education with his former chief, Howson made a memorable retort: 'This is not the kind of school where, if a boy is no good at arithmetic, he is allowed to keep rabbits instead.'

Working from within the system, Howson picked the best of what schools and educationalists within his experience had to offer and he had the courage, and Governor support, to see his plans through. It has been suggested that Howson would not have been a successful Head of a larger school and it may be true. Certainly his system would have failed in such circumstances. He was a realist too. In 1912 he told his audience at the Commemoration of the School's opening 350 years earlier, 'I hope, nay I prophesy, that our curriculum will become the model of the majority of public schools.' And he was right. The other schools caught up and the 'honour system' had outlived its somewhat ambivalent ethical code by the 1930s.

Geoffrey Shaw, the music master who knew when a debt of gratitude needed to be paid, summarised Howson thus: 'A single-minded, brave-hearted man of genius, a great headmaster.' Genius? Perhaps not – but simple justice demands concurrence with the rest.

No.38 in a series of 50 cigarette cards entitled 'School Arms'. Howson would have approved of the publicity – but not the sponsor.

Howson's grave: the south wall of the Chapel.

The Chapel Line.

2

Follow My Leader:

J.R. ECCLES 1919–1935

Howson's sudden death, if not entirely unexpected given his poor health over the preceding two years, presented the Governors with the pressing need to appoint a successor. According to Eccles himself, he had no particular desire to become Headmaster but having seen the shortlist he changed his mind. Doubtless it would have been difficult for the Governors to appoint anyone else once he had made this decision, but he went to Fishmongers' Hall on 21 March to be interviewed by the selection committee. He and one other went forward for a final interview the following week and then he returned to Holt to await the coded telegram from the Clerk to the Governors, Sir John Towse. In due course the word 'Biology' came through and Eccles learned that his application had been successful. Ironically given his academic subject, the word 'Physics' would have meant failure. His first decision, with the Governors' consent, was to remain in Woodlands with Col. Foster taking over in 'The Headmaster's' which became 'Howson's'. J.C. Miller was promoted Second Master.

Like Howson, Eccles was a northerner by birth and as straight-talking as his long-time chief. Born in 1874 in Lower Darwen, Lancashire, he was a Methodist and a Liberal, with and without the capital letter. His father had died before he was 2 and he was devoted to his mother. He was governess-educated at home until the age of 10 enjoying an idyllic childhood before moving to a preparatory school in Reigate, St David's, where he became Head Boy in weeks, 'so I was not altogether unintelligent.' He played in the cricket and football XIs and was much influenced by the 'exceedingly high tone' of the school. He proceeded to Clifton College, Bristol, a school with a fine reputation mainly due to the pioneering work of its great Headmaster The Revd John Percival. Interestingly he went on to the classical side – the modern being 'rather despised at Clifton in those days.' In the sixth form he studied Latin, Greek, History, English and Maths and gave up French in order to study extra Science, Physics and Chemistry under W.A. Shenstone, an eminent scientist who became a Fellow of the Royal Society. Eccles did well. Though not a scholar he was fifth or sixth on the school list ahead of several boys who held awards. He became Head of his House, edited the *Cliftonian* in his final year, gained his First XV rugby cap as a three-quarter and played cricket for the

J.R. Eccles Headmaster 1919–1935.

The first OG Summer week-end after the First World War. Eccles is seated on the steps of the pavilion between the two men in pads.

XI, though he appears to have shown less ability in this sport. He did however enjoy one golden moment when playing for the School against the MCC captained by none other than W.G. Grace, whose son led the school side. Eccles made sixty, was congratulated by the great man, and was awarded his colours. Altogether it was a school career to be proud of, distinguished by reliability, responsibility and high endeavour.

It was his experience as Head of House which decided him to change his intended career from medicine to schoolmastering. At Clifton the Housemaster lived behind the 'green baize door' and hardly ventured into the boys' side, leaving all to his Prefects. Eccles saw this as a dereliction of duty. He believed that Housemasters, in fact all teaching staff, should build up relationships of trust and even friendship with the boys in their charge. In this, as in so much else, he was very much in sympathy with Howson's vision.

In 1893 Eccles went up to King's College, Cambridge, taking a year's sabbatical in 1895 due to a 'breakdown in health' upon which he did not expand. Typically, however, he made full use of this time travelling in South Africa, Australia and New Zealand, which must have been a mind-broadening experience for this earnest, rather naïve young man. He returned to take a First in the Natural Sciences Tripos Part I, for which he was awarded an Honorary Exhibition, and a First again in Part II. Still uncertain as to his future, he 'geologised' for a year in south Wales and then went to Paris to learn French. Returning to Clifton for a term to teach Physics while a former teacher was on leave, he was not happy and went abroad again to Geneva to pursue his French studies early in 1900. In July of that year he revisited his old school to be taken aside by Shenstone, and asked whether he wanted a job. Howson had clearly been writing round the public schools to receive recommendations for the post of Science and Games teacher at his 'new' school. Eccles applied, was interviewed and was offered the post. He declined. Friends, he said, advised him that the job did not sound good enough. However negotiations were reopened and Eccles arrived in Holt on a term's trial. If he was unsatisfied at its end, he could leave. Howson wrote to him after a few weeks: 'Having put your hand to the plough I am sure you won't look back.' He didn't.

Eccles' appointment as Headmaster in 1919 may have been seen as correct or inevitable but it carried risks. He had been, for nearly twenty years, the ideal deputy: loyal, dedicated, energetic, good at detail, a little pedantic, a little ponderous, seemingly without personal ambition and without great vision. He revered Howson and shared his philosophy. He was in some ways similar: devout, high-minded, a scientist, a bachelor, totally dedicated to his job and to Gresham's. He had stature and presence if not Howson's charisma. He was more liberal, perhaps more humane, less authoritarian, certainly less worldly. There was a danger that he would follow too slavishly the path laid out by his old chief, that he would be less alert to the need for change. And the world was changing as the 1920s unfolded. In short, the very strengths which had made him such a superb right hand for Howson might become weaknesses in a Headmaster and might bring down this

The opening of the Thatched Buildings in February 1921.

The Thatched Buildings presented to the School by Eccles in 1921. Later called the 'temporary' classrooms they are still in use today.

enlightened, successful but still new and barely established school.

In many ways Gresham's saw remarkably little change in the ensuing sixteen years. In 1919 the numbers were 242, in 1935 270. It was still, by policy, a small school. The curriculum remained broadly as developed by Howson. The main differences were the introduction of Geography as a major subject, the growth of Biology and the extension of Art and Manual Training. Since the school could not afford the facilities required, Eccles provided them out of his own purse. The Thatched Buildings were erected in 1920 and opened by Sir Arthur Shipley, Master of Christ's College, Cambridge, in the following year. In more recent times, the wooden constructions were referred to as 'temporary classrooms'. They are still giving service as classrooms and, in different, more social guise, as 'Dave's Diner' eighty years on. The emphasis on Natural History, on Societies (augmented in the 1920s and 1930s by such as the Literary and the League of Nations), on a refusal to worship games (there were no matches against other schools during Eccles' Headmastership), remained.

And so did the honour system. Under Howson it had been under attack as an encouragement to priggishness. It came under even greater censorship and scrutiny in the thesis propagated by W.H. Auden in his contribution to Graham Greene's anthology *The Old School*. Whilst acknowledging, albeit rather grudgingly, that he was allowed to make friends where he chose, free to roam the coast and countryside adjacent to Holt at weekends, was never 'bullied or molested' and was 'taking everything into consideration, very happy throughout my time there,' Auden is unequivocal in his criticism of Howson's system which Eccles perpetuated. It was the moral pressure to report a fellow pupil who would not own up to breaking the honour code that Auden pounced upon. 'It meant that the whole of our rural life was based on fear, on fear of the community, not to mention the temptation it offered to the natural informer, and fear is not a healthy basis. It makes one furtive and dishonest and unadventurous. The best reason I have for opposing Fascism is that at school I lived in a Fascist state.' Given that this was 1934, when Hitler had only just come to power and the Spanish Civil War was two years away, Auden cannot be accused of too much distortion. The antics of Mussolini could not disguise the success of some of his social policies and Fascism had its attractions in the economic and political aftermath of the great Depression. There were black shirts in streets closer to home than Rome and Berlin.

A. L. Keith Lucas, who was a contemporary of Auden in Farfield, believed that the honour system by the 1920s was not working as intended (if indeed it ever had). 'It was a more sophisticated age, now more cynical. The boys had their own code of honour. What made the system work was the absence of petty regulations and penalties attached, the illusion of trust in our better feelings, and the fact that the masters were not seen primarily as disciplinarians. They were more like advisors.' Developing his theme with the benefit of hindsight, Keith Lucas continued, 'W.H. Auden said he could understand totalitarianism because he had been at Gresham's. He must either have been over-sensitive or have considered the Honour system as some kind of Orwellian thought control. For Gresham's totally lacked the brutality of totalitarianism. It was much more like living with a Victorian but kindly maiden aunt. She had her little ways – she disapproved of eating sweets and having trouser pockets – but on the whole she didn't interfere very much in our lives.'

J.T. Jones, writing (like Keith Lucas) in the 1990s, was at school during Eccles' final years as Head. His response is equally unequivocal. 'It has been written in informed biographies that the Honour system provided a repressive education. Nothing could be further from the truth: individuality was encouraged to the full, games were not lionised, boys were not bullied by older boys or by staff, and the responsibility for educating him was gradually thrown back to the Gresham's boy in conformity with his degree of maturity. At barely 16 almost half my lessons were study periods'. Jones also refers to the freedom to roam and the outside activities such as sailing, ornithology and sociology. This freedom to explore personal academic interests as well as the sand dunes and salt marshes of north Norfolk was also appreciated by Jones' contemporary A.L. Hodgkin, winner of the Nobel Prize for Medicine in 1963, who commented: 'We were encouraged to read widely and to work on our own, and this I think is the most important thing I learned at School'. It may also account for the number of those who became involved in scientific research after University: David Keith Lucas, Chief Designer of Short Brothers who led the team which developed the Jump Jet; Christopher Cockerell, inventor of the hovercraft; and Ian Proctor whose design of Proctor Spars revolutionised dinghy sailing.

W.H. Auden.

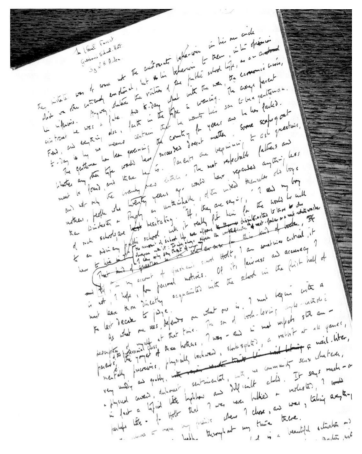

Draft of Auden's critical article on the 'Honour System'.

Neither Jones nor Keith Lucas addressed Auden's main contention about the encouragement to inform on others leading to a furtive and fearful atmosphere. However their descriptions of the honour system in practice put a rather different slant on things. If Keith Lucas experienced a healthy schoolboy cynicism in the 1920s it is likely that by 1935 the honour system was an anachronism. The forthright Bruce Douglas, who became Housemaster of Farfield the year after Eccles' retirement but who had been appointed to the staff in 1921, was reputedly one who had no time for it. In one of several tributes written by OGs on his death in 1963 it is stated that 'he regarded the Honour system as frankly comic.'

The introduction of the honour system by Howson in 1900 had been in Eccles' words 'a bold and original venture.' It had anticipated Baden-Powell's similar plan for the Boy Scouts by nine years. It taught an inner discipline or self-discipline which Eccles thought preferable to discipline imposed from outside. 'There was a great deal of liberty allowed,' he wrote in his pamphlet *My Life as a Public School Master* published in 1948, 'but it was liberty based on loyalty or freedom founded upon trust.' Eccles made great play of his comparison with Clifton where 'our study windows were barred, like the windows of a prison, and at lock-up the doors were all locked. Bars were unknown on our windows at Holt and doors, at what we still called lock-up, were not locked, nor was there any need for it.'

Whatever the rights or wrongs of the system, one cannot doubt the motives nor the integrity of the man who perpetuated it as a matter of sacred trust for it was at the heart of his great chief's work. And whatever the naivety of Eccles' belief in his system and in the essential goodwill of teenage boys, there is little doubt that Gresham's was a remarkably happy and friendly place. Bullying was extraordinarily rare and homosexuality likewise. Auden, who was aware of his own sexuality well before leaving Gresham's, bears testimony to this, and there is no written or anecdotal evidence of any scandal involving boys with boys or boys with masters even though there have been suggestions that some masters may have been inclined towards homosexuality. In a boys' boarding school this would not have been unusual but nothing untoward seems to have occurred. The promise not to indulge in any form of indecency appears to have meant something to the boys of Gresham's.

Under Howson, corporal punishment was rare. Under Eccles it ceased. There is no evidence that he made public proclamation of this but he was opposed to the use of the cane by masters and he certainly did not use it himself. In January 1924 Eccles was invited by the Conference of School Masters and College Tutors to read a paper on 'School Discipline'. With a few alterations 'as a result of questions put to me both in public and in private' he subsequently published the paper 'by request.' Much of the time he is concerned with friendship and trust, the inadvisability of printed rules, the provision of some privacy through studies for all, plenty of scope for hobbies of every kind, and for self-expression to avoid boredom

Woodlands: home to Eccles for thirty years.

Donald Maclean behind his Housemaster in a prefects' group 1931.

which leads to 'undesirable and harmful things.' His case against beating is stated clearly: 'The more I see of the effects of "no caning", the more I am convinced that the absence of caning has far-reaching results. It makes things possible that would not be possible otherwise. It makes for truth and frankness, for loyalty and fellowship. It destroys the sense of fear, for which as a master I have little or no use. It makes for happiness and freedom of development. It enables one to keep more in touch with whatever is going on. It prevents the formation of barriers and breaks down existing ones. We need never be foes to our boys.'

The continuation of Howson's innovations and Eccles' own overt liberalism paid dividends in terms of recruitment. A glance through the Gresham's register for the 1920s and early 1930s reveals a large number of doctors, academics and businessmen, many from the Midlands and the North, who sent their sons to enjoy the modern education on offer. Many came from London too – with a particularly strong contingent from Hampstead, then very much a liberal stronghold. The decision of Gerard Wathen, Headmaster of The Hall, Hampstead, one of the leading London preparatory schools, to send his son Mark to Holt in 1926 must have been significant. There is no doubt that Eccles, like Howson, was tigerish in his pursuit of bright pupils from distinguished backgrounds, his high-minded and straightforward philosophy commending itself to many. The artist William Nicholson had had to withdraw his son Ben after a short stay because of ill-health but a younger brother Christopher stayed the course. Dr Keith Lucas sent three sons who all became Professors. The grandsons of the great C.P. Scott of the *Manchester Guardian* entered the school as did David Layton whose father, Walter, was an eminent economist, editor of the liberal daily the *News Chronicle*, and later a peer. A Lancashire industrialist, Ernest Simon, who became a Liberal (and later a Labour) MP and was appointed Chairman of the BBC and then Lord Simon of Wythenshawe, sent his two sons Roger and Brian. Brian Simon recalls the occasion when he attended a Liberal rally in Manchester chaired by his father and featuring a blazing speech by David Lloyd George, in company with his Headmaster. Mervyn Roberts was the son of Liberal peer, Lord Clwyd of Abergele, and Michael Lindsay's father (nominated for a Labour peerage by Attlee) was the distinguished philosopher A.D. Lindsay. The Hon. David Kenworthy, son of the tenth Lord Strabolgi, later became a Labour Whip. Harry Hodson, who became editor of the *Sunday Times* in later life, was the son of the Professor of Social Anthropology at Oxford, and then there were the three sons of the Liberal MP Sir Donald Maclean.

The youngest of Sir Donald's sons, and his namesake, was to become one of Gresham's most notorious former pupils. Donald was the perfect schoolboy. He was an outstanding athlete, gaining his colours for rugby, hockey and cricket; he became a School Prefect and won a scholarship in Modern Languages at Trinity College, Cambridge. His flight to the USSR in the 1950s together with Guy Burgess revealed the greatest British spy story of the Cold War years.

Inevitably there has been speculation as to whether any formative influences existed at Gresham's. Certainly there were a number of contemporaries – or near-contemporaries – of Maclean who joined the Communist Party during their youth though not at School. Tom Wintringham was a pupil some ten years earlier. Having fought in the First World War, he joined the Communist Party in 1922 and served in Spain commanding the English Battalion of the International Brigade at the battle of the Jarama River outside Madrid in 1937. His experiences there, however, led to his expulsion from the Party in 1938, and at the start of the Second World War he helped to train home forces in guerrilla warfare at Osterley Park. James Klugman was a direct contemporary of Maclean and also won a Cambridge Scholarship in Languages. There he became joint leader of the University Communist Party and Secretary of the World Student Association. During the War he played his part as a liaison officer with Tito's partisans in Yugoslavia and got on well with Sir Fitzroy Maclean (no relation to Donald) who was in charge of the Mission. Post-war, Klugman remained a full-time officer of the Communist Party, editing the Journal and acting as Education Organiser. Bernard Floud, son of a distinguished civil servant, Sir Francis, was two years younger than Klugman and Maclean, and at Oxford became an active member of the October Club, going to China in 1938 as a representative of the International Student Delegation. After the War he became a Labour MP. Brian Simon went to the same Cambridge college, Trinity, as Klugman though several years his junior. There he too joined the Communist Party and later became President of the National Union of Students. Simon maintains that there was no suggestion of indoctrination of any kind at Gresham's, though there were some stimulating teachers like Denys Thompson who taught his students to be critical in their reading and to think for themselves.

Brian Simon makes the point that it was unsurprising that so many University students shifted to the left politically when the conditions of their lives in the 1930s

The Music Department: Miss Chapman, Walter Greatorex, Hoult Taylor.

forced them to recognise fundamental change. Higher education as taught in the cosy lecture rooms of Oxbridge simply evaded the problems of hunger, rickets in children and the rise of Fascism. Marxism provided the tools for such analysis. No doubt there were plenty of extreme left-wing Etonians who did not emulate Guy Burgess or Marlburians who did not go so far as Anthony Blunt. There is nothing to indicate that any Greshamian accompanied Donald Maclean into treachery, with the exception of Cedric Belfrage, unmasked in 1995 as a wartime NKVD agent whose years at school preceded Maclean by a decade.

No history of Gresham's could be complete without mention of Benjamin Britten. He was not a happy boarder – possibly his late arrival at the age of nearly 15 was a contributory cause – and he wrote to his mother of the miseries of the rigorous and fairly Spartan existence. Unlike Auden, who left three years before Britten's arrival, the sensitive young musician spoke of having been bullied and was clearly relieved to leave a year early, in 1930, having won an Open Scholarship to the Royal College of Music. He never got on with Walter Greatorex whom he did not rate as either teacher or musician – unlike generations of Gresham's boys – although there are reports of concerts in which he shone, often playing viola with Greatorex accompanying him.

He had already performed to considerable acclaim one of his own compositions

Two Gresham's composers: Lennox Berkeley (left) with Benjamin Britten .

Speech Day 1931. J.R. Eccles presents his annual address.

– a piano trio entitled *Bagatelle* – when his final school concert sent the music critic of *The Gresham*, in this case the Revd Frank Field, himself about to retire after twenty-five years on the staff, into paeans of praise:

> The apex of the concert, well placed in the centre of the programme, was the playing of Britten. We have had fine pianists at the school but it is no slight to any of them to place Britten above them all. The interpretation of Raff's *Filensa* alone was enough to establish him as a past master of delicate workmanship, but the *Polichinelle* of Rachmaninoff held me bewildered and spellbound . . . The more the fire and fury, or the leaping and plunging increased, the more rapturously could I have shouted for joy . . .

Later on Britten was prepared to think more kindly of his Gresham's days. Writing in 1945 to Greatorex's successor Hubert Hales, he acknowledged, 'In many ways I am grateful to the school. On the whole I was very happy there.' He referred regretfully to 'mutual suspicion between Mr Greatorex and myself' which meant that 'I didn't get much encouragement or help musically,' though he sent his best wishes to Hoult Taylor and Miss Chapman who was 'always very patient with my scratchings on the viola!' Britten offered to help 'particularly promising boys in some direction,' stated that B.A. Fletcher (by this time Professor of Education at Bristol University) had been 'especially good to me' and concluded that, piano teaching apart, 'in many other ways I remember the school with great affection.' It was not until 1964, however, that he could be persuaded to return, with Peter Pears, to give a memorable recital in Big School.

The strength of the extra-curricular societies was certainly one of the distinguishing features of the period. Though the Shooting VIII began to take part in the Ashburton Shield Challenge and competed against public schools throughout the country, the deliberate policy of encouraging keenness in games without creating an athletic elite so prevalent in public schools at this time meant no inter-school matches. Despite this many OGs gained distinction in hockey where Bertram Stowell played for England, and athletics with Kemys Bagnall-Oakeley winning international honours but missing the 1928 Amsterdam Olympics because, as a schoolmaster at Eastbourne College, he was denied leave during term-time. The attraction of the societies was partly due to the skill and enthusiasm of remarkable members of staff. The isolated geographical position of the school, the long terms and the lack of leave weekends and half terms meant that Gresham's was thrown back onto its own resources even more than most boarding schools of the time. But the list was a long one and each activity made its report regularly in the pages of *The Gresham*. The Debating Society has already been mentioned and was one of the first, dating right back to the early Howson days. One proud and perhaps unique boast was the election in the same year (1927) of Old Greshamians to the Presidency of both the Oxford and the Cambridge Unions, J.P. Price and A.L. Hutchinson respectively. Both undergraduates were invited back to inspire future orators at Holt. Howson had also introduced a series of school lectures and these became features of the winter terms. There were many on travel, on natural history, on adventure. There was Capt. Carpenter VC of the *Vindictive* on the 1918 Zeebrugge Raid, Hugh Walpole on writing novels and George Mallory, most arrestingly, not long before he disappeared with Irving on the final assault of Everest in 1924. J.R. Eccles recorded these highlights and other less enlightening evenings including one by a planter entitled 'Rubber' which began with the assertion that 'The Rubber Growers Association is an Association of Rubber Growers' and continued for near an hour in much the same vein. Eccles himself produced what must have become a somewhat over-familiar exposition, with lantern slides, on the Dolomites and turned the laugh on himself at the OG Dinner in 1933 by quoting a recent Punch cartoon. Two ladies talking: 'Do you know the Dolomites at all, dear?' 'Oh yes, darling, Ronald was at school with one of them.' By the mid-1920s the Literature Society had appeared and the Society of Arts, the Camera Club and the Sociological Society (mainly popular because its members were taken out on all manner of expeditions by charabanc). Pride of place went, however, to the Natural History Society, which included sections on zoology, botany, physics and chemistry, entomology, ornithology, geography, geology and meteorology. The Society published its own annual report in the form of a booklet which included photographs, group studies and individual papers which usually included the finalists of the Holland-Martin Natural History Prize. J.R. Eccles made a point of mentioning boys who had produced such papers in his Speech Day address each year, thereby making sure he balanced the Society aspect of school life with the academic. One winner of the Holland-Martin Prize who was also secretary and editor of the Natural History Society was David L. Lack whose lifelong passion for ornithology was inspired by the proximity of the woods and heaths around Holt and outings arranged to Blakeney Point, Scolt Head and the Norfolk Broads. These interests he pursued at Cambridge at Dartington Hall, where he taught for several years, and later at Oxford where he became director of the Edward Grey Institute. Made a Fellow of the Royal Society for his work in the Galapagos Islands, he afterwards maintained that he might have been 'one of the last to be elected for research done as an amateur.'

Sport was mentioned in the Headmaster's annual report, the OTC, the distinctions of OGs usually at the universities and including the exceptional announcement in 1934 of ten Firsts in the Oxbridge Class lists. Also prominent in the school calendar were the House Entertainments, usually in the form of a one-act comedy or melodrama (a tradition maintained until the present, though threatened by the spreading tentacles of the recently introduced AS examinations), the concerts and, of course, the annual Shakespeare play staged in the Open Air Theatre in the school woods every Speech Day. As one of the very few schools with such a facility, this occasion was reported not just in the local, but even in the national press. Thus W.H. Auden's performance as Caliban in *The Tempest* of 1923 brought his name to the public eye as an actor rather than a poet in his 17th year. E.A.

W.H. Auden as Caliban in The Tempest, *1923.*

47

Robertson's direction in partnership with Shaw's specially composed or judiciously adapted music laid the foundations of a fine tradition continued by Hoult Taylor and W. Greatorex.

Testimony to Robertson's ability as a director and inspirer of actors can be found in the OG News section of the autumn edition of the 1928 *Gresham*. Five former pupils are listed as appearing on the London stage of that season: Charles Daniell in *The Return Journey* at St. James', Geoffrey Gwyther in *Blue Eyes* at Daly's, Sebastian Shaw in *The Moving Finge*r at the Garrick, Bruce Belfrage in *The Admiral's Secret* at the Strand and Patrick Waddington in *Loyalties* at Wyndham's. Shaw, a son of Geoffrey, the Music Director at Gresham's, Waddington and Gwyther, who became the manager of the Comedy Theatre, all enjoyed distinguished theatrical careers. Belfrage moved to the BBC where he became famous as a wartime newsreader.

An example of Eccles' encouragement of any initiatives which might bring Gresham's and its pupils into closer contact with Europe was the week-long visit of a dozen German boys and two masters from the Kaiser Frederick Real Gymnasium in Berlin in October 1929 following up a link formed by a school party under B.A. Fletcher earlier in the year. In March 1931, thanks to further groundwork by B.A. Fletcher during a year-long sabbatical travelling round the world, Kurt Hahn came to Gresham's for a brief stay together with a party of twenty boys from his remarkable foundation in Baden, Schule Schloss Salem. The only other school Hahn visited was Harrow. In the following year the first XI hockey team played reciprocal matches at Salem following some interesting adventures in the Black Forest. Hahn's talk to the boys on the political situation in Germany was vividly remembered by those present. The following year Hahn's outspoken views on the new regime under Chancellor Adolf Hitler led to his arrest and eventual flight to Britain. The founding of Gordonstoun in 1934 was the direct result. Brian Simon spent two terms at Salem during this period and vividly recalled the events before and after Hahn's removal from the School.

One other story from the early days of Eccles' Headship deserves to be told in full since it illustrates well his unusually liberal political stance and also his moral courage. Robert Erskine Childers, Haileybury and Cambridge educated, was a clerk in the House of Commons when he volunteered to serve as a horse driver with the Honourable Artillery Company in the Boer War. His diary was published in 1901 and two years later his novel *The Riddle of the Sands* became a best-seller, including as part of the plot a warning to England of the dangers of invasion by Germany. He married the daughter of a wealthy Boston physician after a whirlwind courtship and brought his American bride, Molly, back to London where their son Erskine Hamilton Childers was born in 1905. Childers père had always been close to his Irish cousins, the Bartons, who had a beautiful home in County Wicklow where he had been brought up following his parents' early deaths. Robert Barton became a leading political figure in the Irish Home Rule Movement and Childers was quickly converted as was Molly. Nonetheless, when the War came, Childers flew with the RNAS winning a Distinguished Service Cross and

Erskine Hamilton Childers during his last year at School (1923).

48

Young Erskine Childers (on bicycle) 'daily visited the courts to hear the pleas made for his father's life.'

becoming a Major in the newly formed RAF. By the time young Erskine was ready to leave his London preparatory school, his parents had decided upon the next stage of his education. Though application had also been made to Uppingham and Rugby, Gresham's was chosen because Erskine's parents found much in common with Howson's academic approach, liberal ideas and admiration of creative ability. Howson died as young Erskine entered Woodlands in January 1919, by which time his parents had decided to move to Dublin and Erskine senior had become more deeply involved with Sinn Fein. He later became their Minister of Publicity.

Young Erskine must have become somewhat confused. He lived for two thirds of the year in Norfolk yet in the holidays the whole atmosphere was devoted to severing Irish ties with England. He would like to have joined the OTC but his mother wrote that he could not be 'SF' [Sinn Fein] and go to camp and wear 'that

*Band Competition at
Summer OTC Camp 1930.*

uniform for one moment.' In May 1921 Childers senior was elected one of Sinn
Fein's deputies for Kildare, Wicklow and entered the Dail. Eccles, who had stayed
with the Childers before they left for Dublin, was highly thought of by them. 'He
has a large mind and heart, sympathy and understanding and noble standards,'
wrote Molly Childers. 'There is no school like Holt and no house like his [Eccles']
in England.' Erskine wrote home, 'J.R.E. is always introducing me as a sort of
curiosity, i.e. Sinn Fein, he is awfully nice about it.' Later he commented, 'J.R.E.
has changed sadly, he wants independence but thinks the IRA are all brigands'.
By the summer of 1922 the electors of Kildare had rejected Childers senior who
became a non-combatant staff captain in the IRA editing its war journal. Tensions
rose and Erskine returned for the winter term in 1922 full of apprehension. In
November Eccles called for him and told him of his father's arrest for unlawful
possession of a firearm – a small Colt revolver given to him by Michael Collins. It
was a capital offence. Erskine returned to Ireland and attended the trial. The ver-
dict was inevitable and Childers senior was condemned to death. Appeals for
clemency from both sides of the Irish Sea failed. Erskine visited his father for a
final conversation and was made to promise to work for reconciliation between
English and Irish and urged to convey his forgiveness to those who had signed the
death warrant; a daunting task faithfully carried out. On 24 November Robert
Erskine Childers was executed by firing squad.

Edgar Hope-Simpson was in Woodlands whilst the drama unfolded in Dublin.
He recalls a moving moment when Eccles read out a letter from Erskine Childers
senior. It appeared that he knew he would be executed but had no bitterness
against England and the English people. There was pressure on Eccles to remove
the son of a rebel and a traitor, the Governors receiving a number of letters from
concerned parents. During the previous two years, the British Army had suffered

casualties in a guerrilla war with the IRA. At least three ex-Gresham's officers were 'murdered' including two, David Rutherford and Richard Warren, who had both distinguished themselves in the Great War to the extent of being awarded the MC and Bar before they were 21. But J.R.E. reminded the Governors that Childers had been a decorated pilot in the RNAS and had once visited his son by landing his aircraft on the School cricket field and accompanying him to chapel. Before young Erskine returned to School after a miserable Christmas holiday, J.R.E. gathered together the boys of Woodlands, urging them to welcome him back and reminding them that it would be an unnatural son who would not be loyal to his father – even to his politics. And Erskine earned the admiration of staff and boys by his courage, forgiveness and, outwardly at least, his lack of bitterness.

At the Irish General Election of August 1923, Erskine was prevailed upon to speak at a large rally in O'Connell Street. He protested in his father's name against the arrest of de Valera in a speech given prominence in the British press. This time Eccles found it harder to resist the pressure for his removal. In the end he told young Erskine that he would be allowed to remain until the end of the following summer term, but not into the winter term when Cambridge Scholarships were taken. Furthermore Erskine's younger brother Robert would not be allowed to follow him to Gresham's as had been planned.

However, as Erskine wrote to a young American girl, Ruth Ellen Drew, who was shortly to become his wife, the conclusion of the Gresham's chapter was a positive one: 'It is ending very peacefully and happily, a little life in itself. At first under an overwhelming home sickness, then the screw turning and antagonism and now

Staff 1931.

calm and peace and such happiness as I never knew. When I look back over the past five years they have been very full with a great deal to face. Above all I have learned the real heart of England in a way only a few in Ireland will ever know. For that alone I would have come here.' Gresham's had given him stability, and the tolerance and faith of J.R. Eccles, though questioned by others, was invaluable in sustaining confidence when it was most needed. In 1973 Erskine Hamilton Childers was elected fourth President of Ireland. His predecessor was the man whose photograph had stood on his locker at Woodlands, Eamon de Valera.

Eccles was fortunate to inherit some excellent staff although the War had, inevitably, brought a number of temporary and frankly sub-standard teachers. Back from the front came Lt. Col. J.H. Foster to become Housemaster of Howson's and Second Master in due time. Wynne-Willson remained, the man who 'founded' the Junior House in the town, the Old School House. Frank Field, the Chaplain and also a Housemaster stayed on helping, through his Headmaster brother, Arthur, to forge one of a number of links established with Northern and Midland preparatory schools, in this case West House School. E.A. Robertson and J.C. Miller, respectively the great play producer and first Housemaster of Farfield and Eccles' deputy, died in harness, both in 1928. Walter ('Gog') Greatorex succeeded Geoffrey Shaw as director of Music and stayed, a much-loved figure, until 1936. G.R. Thompson, a sharp Mathematician and Housemaster of Farfield, overcame his physical deformities with the aid of his large and popular Irish wife. C.H. ('Toc') Tyler had been, briefly, Headmaster of Cranleigh before he came to teach Classics and English and served faithfully until 1930. Auden remembered his magnificent bass voice in the classroom: 'From listening to him read the Bible and Shakespeare, I learned more about poetry and the humanities than from any course of University lectures.' Miss Bristow (the 'Bristine') taught Art for quarter of a century. She had studied at the Slade, had been a close friend of the poet Frances Cornford and was recalled with gratitude and affection by one of her students, Robert Medley, artist, stage designer and Royal Academician, when she retired in 1940. 'Pa' Daniel was a popular teacher of Latin who got 11-year-olds to decline 'hippopotamus', and Armand Trévès was one of a number of unorthodox but brilliant teachers who inspired individual pupils to great things. John Hayward, OG, editor, theologist, biographer and bibliographer of French and English literature, recalled Trévès' influence over him during his final year at school when the two would escape on Trévès' motorcycle to have dinner in a Norwich restaurant where the tutorials were carried on in French.

The first appointments made by Eccles in 1919 brought N.P. Birley, a brave and distinguished soldier who only stayed three years and later became Headmaster of King's, Canterbury, and S. Wilkinson who introduced the teaching of Geography to Gresham's. Like Birley, Wilkinson went on to Headship as did the globe-trotting and inexhaustible B.A. Fletcher. Another Head in the making was K.C. Boswell, a brilliant Historian who helped to win a number of top scholarships for his fortunate Sixth Formers. Major W.A.L. Kerridge was appointed to pioneer the Manual Training Curriculum in the new Thatched Classrooms and Arthur Gamble, a long-serving member of staff, made his mark becoming Housemaster of the Old School House and eventually Headmaster of Denstone before retiring back to Norfolk and becoming a clergyman and Rector of Cley. Frank Spencer eventually won promotion as Headmaster of Silcoates School, and with him in 1928 were appointed four men who were to play key roles in the coming years: E.G. Kelly, Australian, Historian, Housemaster of the Old School House and founder of the Kelly Cricket Week; Hoult Taylor, appointed to teach Music but best remembered as a marvellous producer of plays in the Woods, another man who (like Trévès) seems to have been able to inspire the individual; Derek Addleshaw, who lived in Crossways, the house built for bachelor staff, and whose personality made him many friends amongst colleagues and pupils; and L.A.M. ('Max') Parsons, deeply religious, a fine hockey coach (in coat and shooting stick) and Housemaster of Woodlands. A bachelor in the Eccles tradition, his mother processed to House matches with a small boy in attendance carrying rugs. He inspired intense loyalty from his House but was viewed with less affection by fellow Housemasters. Other staff of note appointed by Eccles included Hugh Ramage who taught Zoology virtually to the standard of Part I of the Cambridge Natural Sciences Tripos (he was less successful with younger pupils of lower ability and could be ragged). D.H. Greatwood ('Monsieur Grandbois'), who managed the Languages Department with great success, is remembered for the velocity of his cycle-riding. Denys Thompson, who later became editor with F.R. Leavis of *Scrutiny* magazine, and whose life work was the promoting of 'Use of English' in schools and through School Teacher Associations, was a remarkable and original tutor to those who enjoyed the study of English Literature. 'We were taught,' recalled Nigel Foulkes, who owed much to Thompson (and Greatwood) for his Balliol Scholarship, 'to read for pleasure, to criticise for technique, to distinguish empty rhetoric from passion.' P.A. Smithells was appointed by Eccles to teach Physical Training as a subject which he did with success whilst acting as an unofficial physiotherapist for those with remediable physical defects. He was also a confirmed pacifist and published *World without War: a book for children*.

Perhaps the most interesting of Eccles' appointments was Frank McEachran. Educated at Manchester Grammar School, he won an Exhibition to Magdalen College, Oxford, where he gained a First in German and a Second in French before obtaining a Lectureship at Leipzig University. He joined the staff at Gresham's in 1924. Unexceptional in appearance and quite a reticent figure outwardly (except when laying about him without regard to any rules on the hockey field), he was an inspiring teacher of Modern Languages and capable of extraordinary charisma in the classroom. There were three Open Awards in Modern Languages to Cambridge in 1931 (including those to Klugman and Maclean) and Eccles publicly commended McEachran on Speech Day. He also published at least two books whilst teaching at Gresham's. He had a gift for academic communication and was sought out by boys of a solitary and sensitive nature. A good listener, his somewhat preoccupied and withdrawn air encouraged awkward pupils to open up to him. He also possessed a magnetic enthusiasm

Frank McEachran.

'which generated in silence' according to the Greshamian poet John Pudney, who was to leap to fame with his poem 'For Johnny' written at the height of the Battle of Britain. Boris Ford, later to become Professor of Education at three successive universities, was just one who remembered sitting 'in his Sixth Form during what were called French lessons when he would break off suddenly in the middle of expanding on the economics of Henry George and, gazing upwards in a diagonal way would intone "come let us sit upon the ground" with a long unforgettable descent of the voice at "sleeping slain", or perhaps it would be the whole of Prufrock or a wonderful isolated Greek line . . .' These lines, couplets or whole poems quoted in English, French, German, Italian, Spanish and Greek, with which he interspersed his lessons, were often repeated in unison by the class and long remembered. Benjamin Britten was entranced by the music of words he often could not understand and there is no doubting McEachran's influence on W.H. Auden even if this was unacknowledged by the great man in later years. He was a leading light in the Literature Society and the Society of Arts of which he was President. He was also responsible for the inauguration of the literary magazine *Grasshopper* which continues to this day. His departure was a great loss to the School and came as a result of his idiosyncratic refusal to obey Eccles' injunction against the use of the cane. Apparently this occasional practice was far from harmful to the recipient but a parent complained to Eccles who confronted McEachran. Eccles was at pains to emphasise in his Speech Day address in the summer of 1934 that McEachran had resigned and paid him a graceful tribute describing him as a gifted linguist and an inspiring teacher. Whatever the truth about that interview, his departure was precipitate. An amusing sequel to this affair is told by Richard Sutton, who much appreciated his former teacher to whom he owed his love of French literature and his ability to 'pronounce the language well enough to be taken for a Belgian.' Eric Kelly moved into McEachran's vacant classroom to teach history and, missing the Australian sun, lit a fire in the empty grate. Up the chimney pupils had, over a period of years, secreted numbers of wooden pointers, the weapon with which McEachran had applied mild chastisement. These now caught fire so that, as Sutton recalled, 'we were treated to a series of Guy Fawkes explosions to enliven the doings of Sir Robert Walpole.'

Gresham's loss was Shrewsbury's gain. McEachran became a legend as Head of English there and his *Book of Spells*, as his poetic incantations became known, was published and widely read. During the War the OG poet John Pudney, who was then an administrative officer in the RAF, was chatting to a pilot in a bar in the Air Ministry basement. Richard Hillary, author of *The Last Enemy*, was talking about his writing just before he returned to operational flying and his death. Pudney asked him what had started him off as a writer. 'A man called McEachran,' Hillary replied instantly, 'at Shrewsbury, where I was at school. You would never have heard of the man . . .'

Certainly the most significant staff appointment, however, was A.B. Douglas, who was to serve forty-two years, over twenty as Second Master, a position to which he was promoted in 1942 by Philip Newell on the retirement of J.H. Foster.

Bruce Douglas and family.
A Farfield House group.

Bruce Douglas was a scholar at Rossall and then at Sidney Sussex, Cambridge, where he gained a double First in the Mathematical Tripos. While at school he had been taught Maths by W.F. Bushell who had been inspired by his time as a Master at Gresham's under Howson. It was Bushell who suggested that Douglas should see whether there was a post available at Holt. According to Christine Guedella, Douglas' daughter, Bushell said, 'Go and spend a term there if you can, you will never regret it.' During his time 'The Bird' (a reference to his spectacles and appearance) showed a full range of talents and interests. He was a bulwark of the OTC (having served in France during the last year of the First War) and completed several stints as President of the Debating Society. He coached rugby and became one of the best referees on the East Anglian circuit, was a vigorous hockey player and a reluctant cricketer for the Masters' XI. Together with B.A. Fletcher he organised and accompanied a number of successful school expeditions and tours, during one of which he persuaded some gullible pupils including Dick Bagnall-Oakeley that the Mediterranean was tideless so that they slept in increasingly soggy sleeping bags under the stars on the beach at Perpignan. He taught Mathematics with long-remembered thoroughness, making no distinction in his efforts between the lower reaches of the Fourth Form and the Oxbridge Scholars. And he was a fine Housemaster for the best part of thirty years, first at Kenwyn and then at Farfield, assisted by his wife, the elegant and capable Betty. Serving three Headmasters as Second Master, he found himself Acting Headmaster on two occasions. Through it all he remained imperturbable. He gave advice to Heads and Governors with candour, authority and complete loyalty. Logie Bruce Lockhart was told early on that he (Douglas) considered it his duty to act as his Headmaster's handbrake. He left as a legacy one of his outstanding achievements, the compiling of the School Register which was published, together with a short history of the School written by the School Chaplain C.L.S. Linnell, in time for the quatercentenary in 1955.

Apart from his calmness and common sense, Bruce Douglas is remembered by colleagues, Governors and pupils for his consistency, his humanity, his sharp dry humour, his sayings ('We'll have that talking stopping') and his reference to anything frothy or of little account as 'nonsense'. The 1931 earth tremor remembered by many former pupils was referred to at the time as 'Nature's nonsense'. Douglas was a man of complete integrity as he proved during the two crises which led to his temporary holding of the reins of Headship, of high standards, of understated authority and leadership. Above all, as far as the gaining of pupils' respect and trust was concerned, he was consistent and they knew where they stood with him. Harry Hodson, who was taught by him and later became one of his Governors, remembered the toughness behind the cheery grin and the vigour which persisted to the end. He remembered too, as did everyone, the changelessness over forty years: the full head of black hair, the same strong, stocky frame. 'Those who saw only his modesty and simple goodness and his power to bring the best out of a boy, failed to recognise the far greater debt owed to him by Gresham's.'

Academic standards were high in Eccles' time and many awards were gained, especially in the Natural Sciences (it is significant to note that Auden's Oxford award was in this discipline). In 1931 the Headmaster's report to the Governors

Eccles the OTC officer: seated on the ground (in slouch hat) almost at the feet of Lord Roberts (seated centre) 1905.

Honours Board in Big School.

highlighted 'the largest [Honours List] I have ever had the pleasure of recording' containing three Cambridge College Fellowships (Owen Wansbrough Jones, William Rushton and John Saltmarsh), three Commonwealth Fund Fellowships, eight First-Class degrees, four scholarships won by OGs already at Oxbridge colleges and six by those straight from school. Crowning these triumphs was Benjamin Britten's Open Scholarship at the Royal College of Music. In 1933 he was able to announce that, in recent years, 50 per cent of school leavers had gone on to University at a time when, nationally, of every sixteen candidates taking the School Certificate, only one had proceeded to Higher Education. The Honour Boards in Big School attest to the increasing number of former pupils gaining academic and national distinction.

Eccles had proved an unflagging fundraiser for the Chapel, contributing several hefty donations himself. In addition he gave the Chapel bell with its inscription:

Ring in the Christ that is to be,
Donum Dedit, J.R.E.

At the time of his appointment as Headmaster, the School badly needed new classrooms, especially when Geography, Biology and Manual Training were expanded or introduced. The Governors had not felt able to find the resources. So Eccles gave the money and the Thatched Buildings were provided. After such a lead, the finances for the necessary equipment quickly materialised by subscription. Such generosity was made possible by his private means, but Eccles' total devotion was further tested when the Howson Memorial Library was sited on the playing field opposite Howson's. Sport was important to Eccles as to his boys but the new building would deprive the School of two hockey pitches. Nothing daunted, Eccles promptly purchased five fields to the west of the Waterloo belt totalling 16 acres which now bear his name. As a leaving present in 1935 he provided almost all the funds required for the erection of the squash courts that stand on the edge of that field. Few schools can have had such a generous benefactor.

Other improvements were made to existing Houses, notably to Woodlands, where a new wing brought welcome changing, showering and washing facilities previously situated in outhouses across the yard. The Library, providing in addi-

Field Marshal Sir George Milne arrives to open the Howson Memorial Library 1931.

House evening nets.

tion four lofty teaching rooms for Art, Biology and above all Geography, was designed 'in a modern development of the classical style' and remains an imposing edifice, very typical of its time (1931) but in keeping with the buildings across the Cromer Road. In due course it caught the eye of Sir Nikolaus Pevsner who gave it his seal of approval in his monumental work, *The Buildings of England.*

Photographs of its opening by Field Marshal Sir George Milne, mirroring the great day when the new School buildings were officially unveiled in 1903 by another Field Marshal, Sir Evelyn Wood, cannot conceal from view a very weary-looking Headmaster. Certainly it was Speech Day but the term, in those days, ran on until mid-July. There were more than three years of Headship to go, but the enormous physical exertions with which he burdened himself were taking their toll. His speech paid homage, as ever, to his predecessor's greatness and emphasised the suitability of a Library as a Memorial to him. 'He [Howson] believed in giving boys plenty of spare time and taught them to use it wisely, in such ways as reading, art, music, acting, manual work and natural history. Owing to a room not being set apart for this purpose, reading has not in the past had the opportunities it deserved . . . This need will be fully met now.'

Like all the best long-serving School Masters, J.R.E. is remembered for his 'little ways'. His peculiar diction, strong voice and energetic stride are recalled by Alan Keith Lucas. The familiar bellow was heard as he walked with his brother by Big School: 'David,' it said, 'I like yer.' Alan, who had recently decided against fol-

lowing in his distinguished father's medical footsteps, was in the Biology laboratory when Eccles came in with prospective parents in tow. 'The son of a famous
father,' boomed the voice, 'but a bit of a disappointment if yer ask me.' Keith Lucas
was not a great fan of J.R.E., considering him slightly pompous and puritanical,
warning leavers who were chafing to escape to the excitement of university
against the twin evils of loose women and alcohol. However, when he learnt from
correspondence in the *Old Greshamian* newsletter that it was Eccles rather than
Howson who abandoned corporal punishment, Keith Lucas offered a tribute of his
own: 'We tend to think of him as a disciple of Howson who added little of his
own, but apparently he was a bigger man than we thought.'

H.M. Newton arrived at School towards the end of Eccles' time. He remembers
J.R.E. as 'a bit eccentric' though a very strong character. The threat of being sent
to the Head was a real deterrent; actually to go was a 'terrifying experience.' He
tells one story which even if apocryphal (no confirmation being found of the
major character concerned in *The Gresham*) was certainly credible. The cricket
ground was large and no lines or boundary marks were allowed. This meant that
it was possible for five or six runs to be scored for a single hit. Once when the
first XI was playing MCC the Hon. C.J. Lyttleton was at the crease, having some
time previously captained Worcestershire. He hit the ball hard to leg and ran and
ran. After a while this portly gentleman, red in the face, threw down his bat and
shouted, 'I am not running another bloody foot!' Down the pavilion steps and on
to the field strode an incensed J.R.E. 'Don't you swear like that in front of m' boys,'
he roared. There were occasions in Chapel when by prior arrangement boys
would leave the baritone of the Headmaster to finish a verse alone. A certain
naivety made J.R.E. the author of the occasional comment with a *double entendre*
only apparent to the less high-minded. Referring to the herbaceous borders in
front of Woodlands tended respectively by himself and the matron, Eccles once
remarked, 'I cannot make up my mind which bed I prefer, mine or Miss Scott's'.
G.R. Judd remembered him as 'a formidable personality in every sense of the
word. It cannot be said that he inspired affection but he certainly inspired respect.
I can see him now, his broad figure bustling down the long path from Woodlands
to Big School shouting, "Here, here that boy."' He was a great gourmand, eating
all meals with the boys and then others with his guests on the private side in
Woodlands. New boys were invited to breakfast with him in turn, and he often
took them on a tour of the School including the bell tower of the Chapel. His
observations could be prosaic. On a choir holiday on the Broads he mused about
a passing water lily, 'absolutely lovely – just like a poached egg.' He was a stickler for punctuality and for tidiness. Like many headmasters he was gently ridiculed
for his obsession with picking up litter. His use of grammar was correct though
archaic and he insisted that Physics notes were meticulous to the irritation of
many. Once a fine if fussy classroom teacher, he gave up the Sixth Form in later
years but continued teaching the younger boys Geography in order to get to know
them, but usually bringing in copies of recent newspapers and discussing current
affairs. Although he became a little out of touch, something of an anachronism in

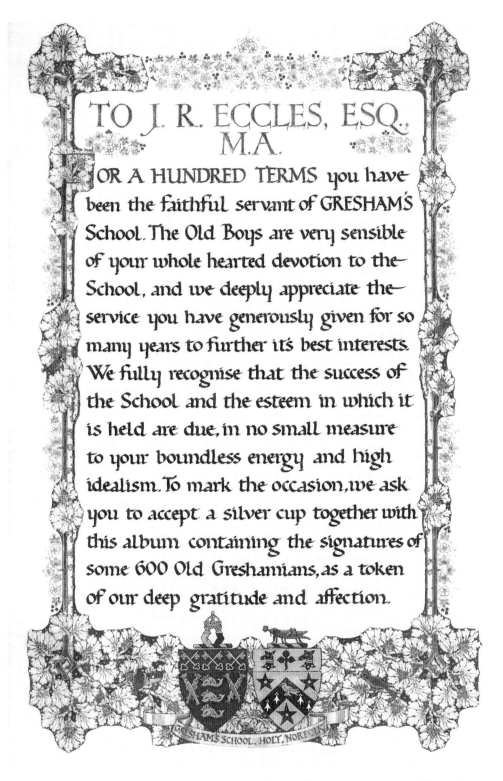

TO J. R. ECCLES, ESQ., M.A.

OR A HUNDRED TERMS you have been the faithful servant of GRESHAM'S School. The Old Boys are very sensible of your whole hearted devotion to the School, and we deeply appreciate the service you have generously given for so many years to further it's best interests. We fully recognise that the success of the School and the esteem in which it is held are due, in no small measure to your boundless energy and high idealism. To mark the occasion, we ask you to accept a silver cup together with this album containing the signatures of some 600 Old Greshamians, as a token of our deep gratitude and affection.

GRESHAM'S SCHOOL, HOLT, NORFOLK

Illuminated address presented to Eccles on completion of his 100 terms. He would not have approved of the misplaced apostrophe.

Howson's prefects 1930 with Lt. Col. 'Joe' Foster, Housemaster.

dress, in speech, in adherence to the Howson tradition, no one doubted even at the end his dominant personality and his complete dedication to the School.

Perhaps J.R.E.'s finest hour came at the London OG dinner in January 1934 when a huge gathering of 260 former pupils, colleagues and Governors celebrated his one hundred terms at Gresham's. He was in his element and even managed a couple of good jokes including one involving the famous Colman family, 'renowned for a certain product which we leave on our plates,' who once invited the formidable W.E. Gladstone to stay at their home near Norwich. On being asked to say grace, the great man first cast his eye around the table. 'Are we all mustered?' he asked, utterly unconscious of any humour. He reminisced about Howson, the Gresham tradition, Old Boys of distinction in all walks of life, former and present colleagues. He paid tribute to the Governors and to the faith and generosity of the Fishmongers' Company in whose magnificent Hall they were dining. Toasts were proposed to the School, to the OG Club and finally to the Headmaster – this by the Revd Harold Fitch who had been Head of School in 1901. A leatherbound illuminated address containing the names of 600 OG subscribers and a beautifully designed hexagonal silver bowl with each side embossed with a picture of the School buildings were presented. Both these splendid mementoes have been handed back to the School for safe keeping.

In his last two years, exhaustion set in and he had a complete breakdown in December 1934, being unable to return for his last two terms. It was as well that he had such men as Joe Foster (who took over as Acting Headmaster), Douglas,

Kelly, Gamble and Parsons to carry on the running of the school without him. He lived on in the house where he was born, The Elms, Lower Darwen, until his death at the age of 82 in 1956. He was far from idle. A life Deacon of Darwen Congregational Church, Chairman of the Committee for the Lancashire Independent College (for aspiring Congregational Ministers), Governor of Silcoates School, a member of Blackburn Education Committee, he published pamphlets, preached, raised money to rebuild churches destroyed in the War and much enjoyed his regular return visits to Gresham's. His obituary in the magazine of his old College – King's, Cambridge – was probably written by Old Greshamian, and History don, John Saltmarsh, who recalled that there had hung in Woodlands a large portrait of Mr Gladstone. 'J.R.E. had all of his hero's liberal idealism with nothing at all of his tortuous complexity. His was a character grandly monolithic, Cromwellian in its simplicity. To some his innate Puritanism was naturally irksome; in subtlety, in humour, sometimes in sense of proportion, he fell short; but none could question his absolute sincerity. "Don't hoard your life," he used to say. "Spend it freely for the good of others." And that he did himself. He lived for his school with an almost monastic self-dedication.'

The Burne-Jones windows in Big School.

The School Band, Newquay.

3

The Road to Newquay:

Philip Newell 1935–1944

J.R.E.'s reign should have ended on a high note. In 1934 at Speech Day he was able to announce a record ten First-Class degrees from Oxford and Cambridge Old Boys and to choose a propitious time to announce his retirement. He tendered his resignation on 15 November to have effect from the end of the summer term 1935. Ill health was specifically not given as a reason. He said he felt it was time to 'hand over the reins to a younger man.' However, he was unable to return to School in January and was destined to remain absent for the whole of the rest of his designated term of office. Colonel Foster, the Second Master since the death of Chambré Miller in 1928, took over the role of Acting Head and the interregnum passed uneventfully enough, much of the credit going to the long-serving modest man who led by example. He was no academic nor visionary. His French lessons, using the modern method of teaching in the language, hardly entered the realms of linguistic brilliance and were doubtless founded upon somewhat limited conversations held with the civilian population behind the front line trenches during the First World War. He was an 'ordinary sort of fellow' by his own observation but extraordinary in dedication and honour, which, added to an eager and kindly disposition, brought him respect and affection. His instinct for leadership was shown in his remarkable army career. Joining up at once in 1914 with only the OTC as background, he rose to the rank of Lieutenant Colonel and commanded his regiment in 1918.

Philip Newell,
Headmaster 1935–1944.

Though Eccles had undoubtedly shown some signs of flagging in his final two or three years, the loyalty that he had shown throughout his thirty-five years to Howson's ideals together with his own strong personality had ensured that Gresham's remained very much in its re-creator's image – for good and for ill. Foster himself had become apprehensive towards the end of *l'ancien régime*. A new headmaster would very likely be an outsider bringing change. Foster was not a staunch admirer of tradition for its own sake and he had not always approved official policy if his common sense told him that what was proposed was not in the best interests of the School, but he was not alone amongst the staff, old boys and even Governors in feeling uneasy as the Eccles era closed. Foster's speech as acting Headmaster was a model of organised reportage with a tribute to J.R.E.,

Speech Day 1936.

praise of teams and coaches for excellent sporting results, especially on the rugby field where every first XV match was won, gratitude to the Governors, and 'our fairy godmother, the Fishmongers' Company,' for funding the restoration of the Chapel where subsidence had threatened its very existence and had necessitated a four-term evacuation, and a special word for Housemasters, their wives and matrons. Of the new Headmaster, who was present, he said, 'I feel sure that under his wise guidance and with the support of Governors, staff, parents and not least the boys, there is a great and glorious future for the School.' E.W. Fordham, Chairman of Governors, after giving due and generous credit to J.R.E. chose a somewhat risky approach to introducing his successor. 'Mr Newell can only be completely successful here if we all back him up.' He warned against the dangers of conservatism amongst all constituents of the School and went on, 'The old ways are not always the best, nor for that matter are the new ones and it is he who makes the right choice between them that makes the best of his journey. And the moral of all this is – if your new Headmaster breaks new ground, don't be hostile; trust him; greet the unknown with a cheer; give it a chance.'

Philip Newell, like his predecessors, had a fine academic record. Educated at Uppingham where he was a Praepostor (Prefect) and a Sergeant in the OTC, he won an Exhibition to Emmanuel College, Cambridge, taking a First in Part I of the Mathematical Tripos and a second First in Mechanical Sciences in 1925. He returned to Uppingham as a Maths teacher and spent two years as Resident House Tutor in the Headmaster's House. He then went to Repton as Maths and Engineering Master and became Head of Maths in 1931. By the time he was appointed to Gresham's he was married with two children. He was, at 32, the youngest member of Headmasters' Conference. Tall and good-looking, Newell made a favourable first impression. Having listened perhaps with some alarm to the Chairman's remarks, he was asked to say a few words after prizes had been

Staff 1936.

distributed by A.B. Ramsay, Master of Magdalene College, Cambridge. He paid tribute to Colonel Foster's work over the past two terms and concluded that Gresham's was 'a magnificent School,' adding 'please God may it so continue.'

The quality of the 1935/6 editions of *The Gresham* is greatly to the credit of its boy editor, Boris Ford, later to become a distinguished scholar and Professor of Education at three successive universities following a stint as editor of *Scrutiny* magazine and of the *Pelican History of English Literature*. Political debates were well attended and there was endorsement for the government's support for the League of Nations and for economic sanctions against Italy in the Abyssinian War. In the Debating Society, the House only just affirmed its belief in England as a free country and defeated heavily a motion that the interests of world peace 'demand that Germany's political and territorial aspirations should receive legitimate satisfaction.' *The Gresham* encouraged a lively correspondence column and instituted a number of competitions including that for clerihews with personalities of the day, including Sir Samuel Hoare, Henry Hall, Dorothy L. Sayers and the editor of *The Gresham*, as subjects. Two examples must suffice:

Confident owl, nervous handler.

> Dorothy L. Sayers
> In answer to our prayers
> Has published cheap editions
> Of her charming eruditions.

And alluding to his playing in Big School assemblies:

> Boris Ford
> Struck a passionate chord
> Which caused the Headmaster
> To pick up the plaster.

There was much reporting of societies, as usual, two articles on textbooks written by Gresham's great eighteenth-century Headmaster John Holmes, reviews of the eighth edition of the literary magazine *Grasshopper,* and a graphic description of a week spent by ten members of the School living in a colliery town in south Wales where over 50 per cent of the male population were unemployed. This article was written by Anthony Sharp, later killed in action during the War.

A significant administrative change was announced in the March 1936 edition of *The Gresham*. Numbers, especially of boarders, had risen during Eccles' last years and Newell was to announce a record roll, 237 (270 including day boys) in his Speech Day address. Consequently the Old School House was to cease to be the Junior House, as it had been since 1905, and, with the construction of a new wing, was to become a Senior House to accommodate the same numbers as Howson's, Woodlands and Farfield. Arthur Gamble was to become Housemaster and Frank Spencer would take on the Junior House in Kenwyn which would be enlarged and adapted for the purpose. It was also announced that A.B. Douglas would begin what proved to be his long and distinguished tenure in Farfield following the retirement as Housemaster of G.R. Thompson. Thus the shape of the school was

Lizard at arm's length.

Extending the Old School House 1936.

altered and remained so until the closing of the Old School House in 1993 and its rebirth as the Pre-Preparatory Department.

Two long-serving members of staff retired in 1936. Both had been appointed by Howson: Walter Greatorex as Musical Director in 1911 and G.R. Thompson the following year. Thompson overcame physical disability to lead a successful Mathematics Department and to be a Housemaster for sixteen years, first in Kenwyn and then in Farfield. To him was entrusted the organisation of the School Certificate Examinations. He lived in Holt in retirement with his wife and daughter who was later killed in a bombing raid whilst serving in the WRNS. Hers is the lone female name on the town War Memorial.

Walter Greatorex, known as 'Gog' or 'Greatox' on account of his formidable size, is best remembered for his hymn tune 'Woodlands' set to the words 'Lift up your hearts, we lift them Lord to thee.' He worked first with E.A. Robertson and then with Hoult Taylor to ensure that plays in the Open Air Theatre gained for the School a more-than-local acclaim and he also gave much to House plays, helping to establish that School tradition. His own playing of piano and organ was exceptional – the assertion by W.H. Auden that in his playing of Bach he was the equal of Schweitzer is well publicised – and he encouraged and nurtured the musical tradition established by Geoffrey Shaw. Essentially a shy and private man, his presence could be intimidating to the young until they realised the warmth within. He could stand aloof from events and give unbiased judgements which caused pupils and colleagues to seek his advice. He possessed unbounded patience, a rich humour and a natural understanding of the young which caused unhappy or lonely boys to seek him out. Stephen Spender, during his brief time in the Junior House, remembered one occasion in particular when he gained considerable comfort from this essentially kindly man.

Aerial picture 1936.

One significant change came not as it should have done in 1936 but in 1937. Howson had been determined to avoid the then prevalent worship of games and had in consequence insisted that matches should only be played against clubs, Cambridge Colleges, the OGs or sides raised by staff or local gentry. In 1936 a hockey match was arranged against The Leys but was cancelled through bad weather. In 1937 history was made when The Leys took the field at Holt against the School first XI, the captain, Chris Todd, receiving a telegram from J.R.E. wishing the team well. The game was lost but, in the first ever away match played by the School the following year, a 3-3 draw was fought at Cambridge – and in the same season the hockey side travelled four hours in a coach to go down 1-3 to Felsted. In that year (1938) a team from Gordonstoun played at the School and lost 0-8. A certain Philip Mountbatten was on the losing side that day.

The south Wales camps continued with small groups staying with unemployed families working on experimental group landholdings (and once being described as 'young men from the Gresham Agricultural College') and trying their hand with the pickaxe at the coalface. Such educational and well-meaning visits met with a mixed reaction in the press and in Parliament, even though they appeared to be welcomed by the local inhabitants. One Welsh miners' MP stated categorically that 'we don't want any more public-school boys coming down here to teach us how to employ our leisure – we don't want leisure, we want work.' In the Easter holiday in 1937 a fortnight's camp was organised under the auspices of the Anglo-German Circle. Eight Gresham's boys, eight Germans and eight unemployed Midlands lads joined together for the purposes of 'promoting better understanding between classes and nationalities and of accomplishing a job of work to which all

Above and below: Anglo-German Work Camp, 1937.

Extreme left is D.W. Thompson, killed in action.

High Street, Holt.

Lilywhite (1932) Ltd Sowerby Bridge.

Holt in the 1930s.

make a contribution.' Arthur Gamble was Camp Commandant and the work involved the making of a path leading from the rugby field to the projected new Sanatorium beyond Farfield and adjacent to Waterloo Farmhouse. *The Times* took an interest in this initiative describing the discussions involving talks on education, ideologies and unemployment, and expeditions to local stately homes, Colman's works, Norwich Cathedral and a football match. M.J. Youngs, one of the Gresham's boys, remembered the National Socialist convictions of all the German students who were slightly older than their English counterparts and who were inevitably members of the Hitler Youth. This was a theme taken up by *The Times*: 'It is difficult to estimate the positive results of the camp as a whole. One thing has been deeply impressed upon their English friends – the passionate earnestness of the German youth. Perhaps it is not too much to hope that they, in their turn, may have learned something of a more tolerant attitude towards those who, while working for the same ends, yet cannot agree as to the method.' Youngs also recalled the visit paid by the Germans to Weybourne on hearing of a First World War German pilot who had crashed and was buried in the churchyard. They laid a wreath in a solemn ceremony and gave the Nazi salute. One evening they all went to the cinema in Holt to try to lighten the mood by watching Charlie Chaplin in *The Great Dictator*. Unfortunately the film included a hilarious impersonation of Hitler complete with appropriate moustache. Cocoa and biscuits that night were consumed in sombre silence. A visit to Hitler's Germany in the same year by N.G. Foulkes (soon to win a major Scholarship to Balliol, Oxford) described the organisation, the uniforms, the indoctrination, the notices barring Jews from cafés, swimming pools and public buildings, the parades, the flag-waving and the dominance of the police and the Nazi Party in all things. Foulkes acknowledged the efficiency of the regime, the social improvements, public works and physical fitness but was less impressed by the intellectual and cultural aspects of the country. Nonetheless a debate attended by almost half the School in November 1937 carried a motion by 71 votes to 54 that 'this House wants Peace at any Price.'

The national and European situation notwithstanding, Philip Newell was able to deliver favourable and optimistic reports from 1937 to 1939 recording considerable academic success. The school had featured in one of a series of articles on 'Britain's Public Schools' in the *Daily Mail* in June 1938. The writer, John Rickman, made much of the Howson tradition and relayed the impressive statistics (for a school of only 270 boys from 9–18) that in the past ten years, forty-three Oxbridge scholarships had been won and fifty-four First-Class degrees awarded. Newell also noted the completion of a number of projects, many of which added greatly to the facilities of the School. The Eccles portrait, by Hugh Rivière, was unveiled and hung in Big School and this was quickly followed by the panelling which now bears the names of so many distinguished alumni. Newell spoke of the then current ten-year building programme beginning with the Library in 1931 and including the extension to the Old School House and Kenwyn, the belated opening of the squash courts and the building of the new Sanatorium (1938). The foundations of a new Gymnasium were to be seen near the squash courts. Chairman Fordham was able to blow the trumpet of the Headmaster and staff as a result of the Board of Education Inspectors' Report on a four-day visit in 1937. The previous summer had seen one of the great acting performances still recalled by those fortunate to have been present when Michael Aldridge, who went on to a distinguished stage career, took the part of Hamlet. He followed it up the following year with Othello but that was not all for in 1939 Hoult Taylor directed *Twelfth Night*. Of this production Ben Travers, comedy writer, Fishmonger and Governor, wrote in his autobiography, *A-sitting on a Gate*: 'It was at Gresham's that I saw Michael Aldridge play Sir Toby Belch in the Annual Shakespeare Play to provide me with the most salient example of stealing a show in the whole of my career.'

On Speech Day in 1939 when the Chief Guest was the one time Gresham's runaway Sir John Reith, first general manager of the BBC, Philip Newell spoke of an earlier Sir John's good sense in establishing his School in Norfolk – 'Ideal from the point of view of Air Raid Precautions; an area to which children would be sent in time of emergency.' Under the guidance of Major Kerridge, each House with varying degrees of difficulty had constructed its shelter for up to eighty people complete with electric light, duckboards and a corrugated iron shell with soil, stones and turf to provide a three-foot-thick roof. The blackout was completed by the time the first East Enders arrived. They came by bus and slept the first night on tombstones in the Churchyard in Holt. Forty boys and girls spent two nights in Howson's dormitories and three children remained on the private side, with the Head's family, when the others moved to their billets. These three had never seen pyjamas before and slept not in but under their allotted beds on the first night, not through fear but because that was the way they had always slept – under their parents' bed. The School entertained troops and evacuees putting on the comedy

Digging the first turf for the Squash Courts 1936.

Headmaster and family visit the site of the New Sanatorium (now Britten House).

Above and below:
East End evacuees 1939 .

Tons of Money in Big School and scrubbed and cleaned an old Victorian villa in the town to serve as a sick bay for the new arrivals. At Christmas a party was given in Big School with a 30-foot tree and a present for every East End child.

Things were looking up in early 1940, the phoney war was at its height and some evacuees trickled home. Then in May 1940 as the School assembled for the summer term Hitler invaded the Low Countries. The ensuing weeks were full of the stories of Allied retreat, the German armies advancing towards the coast, and the desperate plight of the British Expeditionary Forces on the beaches at Dunkirk. The Governors took advice from friends in high places, including Sir Harold Scott, Head of the Ministry of Home Security, who was father to a Gresham's boy. It was still hoped that the School would remain at Holt and invitations to Speech Day were sent out early to emphasise the point. Nevertheless the Governors thought it prudent to advertise for accommodation for a boys' boarding school in a 'safe area in the west of England or Wales.' There was little response. Meanwhile, the Clerk to the Governors, Cyril Hooper, heard that hotels in Newquay, Cornwall, were finding times hard and that two might be available. Colonel Foster and Ernest Dyson, the Bursar, investigated. 'Essentials satisfactory,' they reported. The staff were summoned and asked in secret to prepare lists of essential equipment whilst the Governors wrote once again to the parents that the policy remained to stay at Holt. On 31 May the Governors were advised that an invasion was a serious risk. Sir Vincent Baddeley (or 'Vinbad the Sailor' as Ben Travers called him) had held high office in the Admiralty and his information from the First Sea Lord was that

Building Air Raid Shelter at the Old School House, 1939.

the deep water off Weybourne made that a possible bridgehead. A letter was sent to parents that boys would be sent home on 4 June. On 13 June the Headmaster wrote telling parents of the decision to evacuate the School to Newquay. Each boy should bring a cotton sunhat. The story of that extraordinary logistical operation is told, together with ensuing events, in a small book published in 1987 and written by Philip Newell, then in his 80s, and by Bernard Sankey who had been appointed in 1936 and saw out the whole of the Newquay period, returning to Holt to become Housemaster of Farfield and Second Master to Logie Bruce Lockhart. Surprisingly few of the 270 pupils who attended the School in May 1940 were withdrawn and 236 assembled in Newquay on 25 June 1940.

Hugh Ramage's Natural History Society Report encompassed the migration from north Norfolk to Cornwall (the Cornish apparently referring to Norfolk and Suffolk as 'The Far East'): 'Egg-laying at Blakeney Point was just in full swing when we had to leave. We were very sorry to have to make a break in the records from Salthouse, the Heaths and the School Woods, which have been regularly kept for so long. However, our first glimpse of Pentire Point West and the Gannel, thoroughly reassured us; and we soon realised that we had come to a place with a fauna and flora as varied as we could wish for.' The School occupied two hotels, The Bay and The Pentire. The Bay faced the lovely Fistral Beach and was relatively sheltered; The Pentire was 200 yards away – on a gradient of 1 in 4, uphill. Within a week of arrival, a hundred boys crammed the rickety external iron fire escape to watch Spitfires from RAF St Eval shoot down a 'tip and run' Heinkel Bomber attacking the Anti-Aircraft Training Post at Penhale. No bombs fell near Holt where the army took over the School buildings on 12 July.

J.S. Dodd, a languages teacher and talented amateur artist, came close to arrest. The censor had intercepted correspondence with a friend in his native Ireland. It contained a map with crosses marked 'recommended'. Fortunately the

Last Days at Holt.

Boys building the Chemistry Laboratory.

Superintendent of Cornish Police was himself a fly-fisherman and accepted that a fellow enthusiast had simply been sharing his knowledge of the best freshwater stretches.

Dormitories, dining halls, studies and classrooms were somehow created in the hotels or adjoining huts. There was no Chemistry lab at first. The gas supply ended some way away. But the local company gave permission and gangs of boys dug up the road to create an extension and then built their own laboratory. For playing fields the Schools leased three moderately level fairways on the local golf course – until then the beach gave recreational space and the cliffs (illegally) and rocky coastline provided hours of exploration. Wartime rationing and insufficient facilities were problems successfully overcome by Sylvia Newell and her dedicated team of caterers. The OTC was reorganised with a Junior Section and a more difficult proficiency exam would take a boy straight to Officer Cadet Training Unit (OCTU). The School provided a squad for the Home Guard. Rifles were in short supply but Dick Bagnall-Oakeley, ex-Headboy and already renowned as a teacher of games, natural history and geography, started to build a Shooting Eight. After he had inspected the results of a burst of rapid fire, he reported: 'The men who are to defend England have, this morning, shot away the supports of the targets.' OTC Dawn Patrol of the Headland was a regular duty. Rifles were loaded, safety catch on. On return, ammunition was returned to the stores and weapons inspected. On wet days this was done indoors. This led to the incident of the 'Bishop's bullet'. A supposedly defective rifle caused the firing of a live round which passed through the floor of a guest room and exited through the ceiling. The occupant of this room was 'quietly reading morning prayer' at the time. He was John Daly, OG, Bishop of Gambia and the Rio Pongas.

Hoult Taylor produced, on the last three nights of the first summer term at Newquay, *The Merchant of Venice* in the local Repertory Theatre. Because of a last-minute crisis, he took the part of Shylock himself. In December, with the help of Hubert Hales, the Music Master, he produced *The Beggar's Opera* with a cast of forty. The Band was re-started and became a feature of Newquay life for years to come. On Saturdays it marched for practice through the middle of Newquay past a line of hotels on the seafront. The windows of one, The Bristol, were always packed with eager faces: the girls of Benenden School. The Drum Major remembered one embarrassing moment when he attempted to toss his mace over a telegraph wire and badly mistimed its re-entry. Pigsties provided a new project for budding swineherds, manure for the Bay gardens' marrows and a smell far worse than the Chemistry lab. Works, public and charitable, were organised by Max Parsons and money received went to Defence Bonds and the Newquay Scholarship Fund aimed at broadening the intake of pupils. A.B. Douglas hit upon an ingenious way of saving himself time, energy and the threat of pneumonia whilst undertaking his increased load of hockey umpiring. He drove his car up to the touchline and, using his horn as the whistle, enlightened the players as to the direction of a free hit by means of his indicators which, in those days, took the form of 'daggers' raised and lowered at the flick of a switch.

Throughout all this activity, which helped the people of Newquay quickly to take the Gresham's community to their hearts, academic standards remained high and awards were won to university. Spirits and morale were also buoyant but serious concerns had to be addressed by the Headmaster and Governors. At their core was finance. The School already owed the Court of the Fishmongers' Company £5,000 borrowed in 1937 to fund new buildings including the Sanatorium. With a full School this was being paid back over a period of years. Edward Fordham, the Chairman, asked the Company to agree another interest-free loan of £5,000 for the move and the first year at Newquay. The Company graciously agreed to this and to other financial commitments including upkeep of staff property in Holt. The annual rent of the two Hotels was nearly £4,000 but the army only paid £2,500 for the School and its land. A further blow was the drop in the School's rental income, mainly from London properties. Fishmongers' Hall itself had been badly damaged soon after the Blitz began on 9 September 1940. Now the bombing severely dented the School's endowment. The Fishmongers used to hand over £5,750 to the Governors each year. It was calculated that the total income from the Gresham's Estate by 1942 was only £3,850 p.a. More than ever the School needed to maintain its numbers but this was simply not possible. 236 pupils had joined the School at Newquay in the summer term of 1940. The winter term of 1940 began with 233, a remarkably good figure in the circumstances. In September 1941 the roll stood at 226, including a growing number of Newquay day boys. In 1942 there were 199 boys, and by the summer term of 1943, 196. Only 180 assembled in the autumn of 1943 and by now the anticipated loss for the year was between £4,000 and £5,000 with no prospect of beginning to repay the Fishmongers' loans. Staff were affected by financial wranglings as to allowances for boarding housemasters and

War Weapons Week, Newquay.

John Williams takes the beginners in the Open Air baths after the War. Williams served from 1938 to 1972 and was Head of the Junior School.

Peter Brook, later to become an acclaimed theatre director (middle row second from left) outside the Bay Hotel 1941.

salaries. The Headmaster's own remuneration was a sore subject and Newell fought hard for his senior staff whilst trying to maintain sufficient full-time and active teachers to ensure that extra-curricular activities and games supervision were maintained. Relationships became strained as the months went by.

As early as the autumn of 1941 the Headmaster had petitioned the Governors about a rapid return to Holt but the army was not to be moved. The Regional Commissioner, Sir William Spens, was adamant and remained so. There is an old Norfolk saying: 'He who would Old England win, must at Weybourne Hope begin' – but even when the serious threat of invasion began to subside in 1942, there was no sign of an early return despite the best efforts of individual Governors with influence in politics and the High Command.

Younger staff were called up in the first months of War: Paul Colombé, John Williams, Jan Day, Xenophon D'Aeth, Dick Bagnall-Oakeley, Reynolds Stone. Sergeant Wright died suddenly in December 1940; a grievous blow as the School lost a loyal, many-sided man who had served faithfully for twenty years. In 1941 Arthur Gamble, a giant of Gresham's, was appointed Headmaster of Denstone. Eric Kelly succeeded him as Housemaster of the Old School House. Ernest Dyson was promoted to Bursar at Fishmongers' Hall and then became Registrar at Southampton University. He had served the School with distinction for well over twenty years. That great teacher of English, Denys Thompson, gained his Headship at Yeovil as Frank Spencer was to do at Silcoates the following year, taking his excellent wife Dorothy – a double loss for the teaching staff. Hoult Taylor, musician, producer, director and friend to many Greshamians of all ages, took a job at the BBC. A.C. Candler, a physicist of stature, took a post in industry and Colonel Joe Foster, by now past retiring age, finally departed after thirty-six years. He had played sport against the School in Howson's first term and had joined the staff in 1906. Now he was going home – to Holt. All regretted his departure, many envied him his destination.

Although there were a number of capable replacements, including Richard Stoney-Smith and Laurie Taylor who were to serve the School well for many years, there were others whose stays were less lengthy and distinguished. Quite simply it proved impossible to recruit the calibre of staff which the School had come to expect before the War – well as the Old Guard performed, with Bruce Douglas now Second Master and the likes of Kelly, Parsons, Ramage and Addleshaw. The Headmaster's hands were tied financially too. Gresham's had never paid good wages, indeed the salary scale was shown in a pre-war HMC survey to be at the bottom of the Conference list. Scientists, especially, were at a premium and Philip Newell was fortunate to enlist Oscar Hughes who stayed from 1940 to 1944. He had multiple sclerosis and he died shortly after he left the staff. He was paid at the bottom of the scale despite his brilliant academic record and he could not handle much of the chemical apparatus, but he could teach and proved an admirable stand-in for Jan Day, away in the army.

As the New Year dawned in 1943 the burning question was how to get the military out of the School buildings. It was suggested that the Ministry of Education might help as they had done when Malvern had returned in 1942 from exile in Blenheim Palace only to be turned out again. The Governors agreed that an approach should be made to R.A. Butler who was preparing the first stages of his 1944 Education Act. His letter to the Chairman is worth reproducing in full since it sets out the difficulties faced by all Schools then prevented from returning to their premises by requisition and the quartering of troops. He also refers to the School's excellent Inspection Report of 1937 and to its importance to the East Anglian educational scene:

Parade dismissed outside the Pentire Hotel Newquay 1941.

Pentire Hotel (photo by Eric or Duncan McCuaig, both killed flying with the RAF).

The Board of Education
14 Belgrade Square
South West 1

March 27th 1943

Dear Mr. Fordham,

I understand that the Governing Body of Gresham's School, Holt, are likely to be approaching the Director of Quartering at the War Office in the early future on the possibility of bringing the School back to Holt and that an expression of my views might help in the consideration of this case.

The number of public schools whose premises were evacuated early in the War and which are still prevented from returning by occupation of their premises is small – the main instances being Felsted and Bromsgrove, and Gresham's. In all three cases the school depends for its prosperity largely on its local connection and in the case of Gresham's the serious results of its prolonged exile at Newquay are clearly demonstrated by the drop in numbers of pupils from 240 in 1940 to 195 at the beginning of the current term with the certain prospect of a further decline unless something is done to arrest it. The Fishmongers' Company, who are Trustees of the School, are, I understand, financially handicapped by the very serious loss of income due to War damage and are quite unable to face the rising annual deficits of school maintenance, which inevitably result from the decline in numbers.

Fistral Bay, Newquay.

I find that on the occasion of the last full Inspection of the School in 1937 the Board's Inspectors formed an exceptionally high opinion both of the efficiency of the School and the qualities of the present Headmaster. It cannot therefore fail to be a matter of great concern to us at the Board that these high standards should be threatened by the handicaps of existence under makeshift conditions at Newquay. But what is of far greater moment is the disastrous effect that declining numbers and dwindling resources may have on the ultimate prospects of the School and even on its chances of survival.

Unless some means can be found of restoring to the School its own premises I am afraid that the situation will go from bad to worse and I am convinced that irreparable harm would be done to education in East Anglia and in the country at large if this School were forced to suspend its excellent work. I earnestly hope therefore that the School may be allowed at an early date to re-occupy at least so much of its own premises as will enable it to return from Cornwall to Norfolk.

Yours sincerely,

Signed R. A. Butler

Bernard Sankey's son Alan in defiant pose.

A copy of this letter was sent to General Lammie, Deputy Quarter Master General, to little effect.

By the summer of 1943, with the rapidly falling roll and mounting debts, the School and its Headmaster were under grave pressure. The Fishmongers' Company had made it clear that their loss of corporate income through War damage meant that they were unable to continue to subsidise the School. There were rumblings of discontent within and without the School despite the apparent activity and enthusiasm. The Governors discussed matters amongst themselves and then with the Headmaster who eventually insisted on a vote of confidence, failing which he felt it incumbent on him to resign. Despite signs that the worst was now over and that the coming second front would mean that a return to Norfolk would be possible in the foreseeable future, that vote of confidence could not be given. With the help of Sir Vincent Baddeley, and through his own initiatives and ability, Philip Newell obtained a senior post in the Admiralty effective from 6 March

Bathers studiously ignoring a warning.

OTC Inspection.

1944. The staff and pupils were informed on 17 February and in his letter to parents Newell wrote that he felt able to leave the School since 'our corner now seems to have been turned.' Tributes were paid to the School and by association to the Headmaster by the Lord Lieutenant of Cornwall Colonel Bolitho and by St John St Aubyn, High Sheriff, who thanked the School 'for all it has done for us during your sojourn in Cornwall. I have been struck by the public-spirited attitude and discipline which have been shown by your boys on the occasions when I have met them.' And so, on the evening of Sunday 5 March the Headmaster and his family left for London. The assembled staff and pupils watched them go with general regret. 'The last goodbye came that evening at half-past eight,' wrote the editor of *The Gresham*, 'It might have been a scene from a book; the moon, the car, the school lining the road. We gave him three cheers and the last scene was that of the tail-light of the car disappearing down the road into the darkness.'

All schools which were evacuated during the Second World War faced similar problems to Gresham's and those which travelled furthest generally suffered most heavily. Of the seventeen other members of the Association of Schools evacuated to Cornwall, four came from London and the rest from Kent, Sussex and Hampshire. Not one came from a distance comparable to Gresham's. All saw falls in their rolls though some like King's, Canterbury recovered to their former size before returning. A fair comparison may be drawn with The Leys, Cambridge, which was requisitioned in 1940 by the Ministry of Health as a hospital and took over the Atholl Palace Hotel in Pitlochry, Scotland, until 1945. The roll fell from 230 to 170 but rapidly recovered to its pre-war numbers on return to Cambridge. Another example, Westminster School, reads like the roll after the Charge of the

Helping the War effort: potato picking.

View of Newquay during the War.

Light Brigade at Balaclava (the fateful order for which was given by an OW – the Commander-in-Chief Lord Raglan) – 370 Westminsters left London in 1940 for Herefordshire and only 130 returned in 1945.

The School recovered as the buildings were restored. In 1940 before the move to Cornwall Gresham's numbered 270; by December 1944 the roll was 181; a year later, by now re-established in Holt, there were 286 pupils. But whereas Newell became a casualty, Gerald Humphrey of the Leys and John Christie of Westminster both led their respective schools back to barracks.

Philip Newell served the Admiralty for twenty years as Principal, Assistant Secretary and finally Under Secretary retiring with a CB. But his last official appointment, as Director of Greenwich Hospital, probably gave him the greatest satisfaction. In 1937 he had been asked to serve on a Committee of Inspection to advise on the Royal Hospital School which had recently been transferred from Greenwich to newly built accommodation at Ipswich. Now he could devote himself to improvements in education and to securing the future of that School as a provider of education for the sons [and later daughters] of seafarers through developing its resources of land and investments. In a *Times* obituary describing a distinguished career the following sentence seems particularly apt: 'Although he was an administrator of considerable ability who might well have risen even higher in the Civil Service if he had entered it at an early age, Newell remained at heart a School Master.' In 1990 at the age of 87 Philip Newell returned to Gresham's to preach a sermon in the Chapel on the fiftieth anniversary of the School's evacuation to Newquay. He died a few weeks later.

The last post, Newquay.

Natural History Society members helping to provide nesting sites for fulmars on Weybourne Cliffs in March 1948.

4

Return and Restoration:

MARTIN OLIVIER 1944–1954

Martin John Olivier was 44 years old, a bachelor, who had been an Assistant Master at Rossall School for the whole of his twenty-two years' teaching career to date. He had been a good athlete himself and was a highly successful coach. Rossall athletics teams had an outstanding record in the north of England and at the White City. Furthermore, he had a reputation as a sports writer and had been given leave to cover the 1936 Olympics for the *Yorkshire Post*. He was to repeat this role at the 1948 London Olympics for the *Eastern Daily Press*.

Martin Olivier was highly recommended on the episcopal grapevine and the Governors took the unusual step of appointing without public advertisement. Speed was of the essence and perhaps it was felt that to go through a long process of interviews was inappropriate. The Second Front was rumoured to be imminent and a return to Holt might be authorised at any time. Bruce Douglas was put in charge pending the appointment and the Governors looked at only two other possible candidates, both Old Greshamians and one already a Headmaster. The unusual process was cleared with the Board of Education and Olivier's appointment was made public. Douglas' Speech Day address made clear how many friends had been made in Cornwall but how much everyone at the School looked forward to the return to Holt, though the time was not yet settled. He tried to outline a picture of the School for the incoming Headmaster, who was present. Gresham's was a School characterised by 'an absence of fear and an atmosphere of tolerance.' Work was important and boys were encouraged to learn to study by themselves without being driven. Games had been summed up recently by the Chairman – 'there is nothing so important and nothing so unimportant.' Boys were trusted, though not blindly. Mr Olivier was not to deduce that he was to 'take over the duties of an Archangel in command of a company of angels.' But Gresham's was a happy School and an active School looking forward to a future 'even greater than our past.' In a letter dated 20 November 1944 the Clerk to the Council of Newquay wrote to the new Headmaster informing him of a unanimous resolution expressing keen appreciation of the many ways in which the School, masters and pupils had entered wholeheartedly into the corporate life of their community: 'Throughout the period the School has been in Newquay it has always been more

Martin Olivier, Headmaster
1944–1955.

than willing to respond to any appeal for assistance.' Particular mention was made of 'salvage drives' and the many occasions when the band had turned out for parades and savings weeks. Help with the Youth Movement was also much appreciated. It was a fine testimony but it was time to go home.

The exile in Cornwall had lasted over four years and the grounds and buildings back at Holt showed signs of neglect and occupation by the military. The Eccles Field had been turned over, once more, to agricultural use in the form of potatoes. The whole School was set to pick stones and other alien objects on a House basis and it was several years before Eccles' gift rang once more to the sound of hockey sticks and cricket bats. The Houses and classroom areas took less time and trouble and the Library had been used simply for storage. The one area of seemingly wanton destruction was in the School woods where an assault course had been constructed (the remains of which were still clearly visible in the 1980s) and shrapnel embedded in trees testified to their use in training recruits to throw hand grenades. The Theatre was destroyed and it took five years to reconstruct it. Major W.A.L. Kerridge retired in 1946 but he continued to oversee the work together with his young assistant 'Jumbo' Burrough. Once again the boys and staff combined as they had in 1907 to create the marvellous 'Greek' Theatre where the annual Shakespeare play – and the speeches and prize-giving – could take place in a matchless setting.

From the Governors' (and the Bursar's) point of view the most encouraging aspect of the first eighteen months back at Holt was financial. From the lowest point of 180 in the autumn of 1944 the roll soared to 286 in 1945, and 326 in 1946, fifty more than the previous highest total in 1934. Many of these additional pupils were too young to enter the main School and this very soon placed a strain on the accommodation in 'old' Kenwyn. In September 1945 Crossways, built at the end of the First World War as a house for bachelor teaching staff, was converted into a second Junior House under the avuncular eye of Derek Addleshaw. The accumulated debt from the wartime years was soon under control, despite a lack of co-operation from several Government departments. The other major post-war bonus was the return of the warriors – Dick Bagnall-Oakeley, Paul Colombé and Jan Day who were to be amongst the stalwarts of succeeding decades.

Few who experienced it will easily forget the winter of 1947. Martin Burgess, later an expert horologist, then a 16-year-old in Farfield, wrote a graphic description:

As the small train from London with the Gresham's coach pulled into Holt Station that mid-January the dusk was just falling. There was the usual smell of coal smoke and hot oil from the engine and the first few snowflakes were just starting to fall. The walk with suitcase up the back lane, up the Cromer Road, up the Farfield path with the lights shining out from the house showing up the snowflakes, was usual. Little did we know what was going to happen. The winter cold did not let up until well into March. The really serious snowfalls did not come for about another ten days or two weeks however. A huge high-pressure centre with circular isobars packed close together settled onto northern Europe like a great cold boil. This brought deep cold and strong Easterly winds to North Norfolk as more and more air poured into the system from the upper atmosphere like matter falling into a black hole: conditions intensified, became more established. Such a system was not going to shift.

It was only two years after the war and fuel all over Europe was very short. The School could not be heated. Heating in any case was by gravity-driven hot water from solid-fuel boilers and quite insufficient for what was needed. The first building to go was the Chapel. It was hardly used throughout that term. Periods were held in full overcoats and scarves and gloves. If it happened now the School would be closed but such a step was not even thought of then. In any case the roads were blocked and there was little or no petrol and there were no gritting and salting lorries. Even the railway was blocked for two weeks and Holt was cut off from the outside world: no letters, no papers, no new supplies. There were no mechanical diggers then and no snow ploughs but some clearing was done with spades. The bus from Sheringham did get through eventually, single lane between walls of snow 12 feet high slithering from side to side and bouncing off the sides.

One day the School was called out to dig out a farm, or was it a small village? Hurrah! No periods! In the afternoon everyone prayed there would be periods, it was so cold. A man had died. The people dug from one side and the boys from the other and when they met they carried him out through the path over the snow.

The sea froze. Ice floes could be seen grinding off the Norfolk coast. It was a bad time for the birds, millions died. We saw dead gulls hanging upside down from the telephone wires, their feet frozen on. Two Farfield boys brought back a sick gull and attempted to save it in their study. It was a brave attempt but after a few days it died. They also found a dead seal on the coast, frozen onto the ice. They skinned it and tried to cure the skin. It was pinned out on a board in the drying room for weeks. On at least one clear night we

Skating on the school pond.

saw the Aurora Borealis from the Farfield tennis court, like waving net curtains thousands of miles high. Fantastic!

Farfield was not so fantastic, it was very cold, it has too many windows. I was in a study at the end of the corridor in the southwest corner and the hot-water pipes did not even get warm there and there were three windows and two outside walls. Nowadays, boys would order proper Arctic gear from home but then there were not such things to buy and in any case, all clothes, even knitting wool, were rationed. There was little anyone could do. I slept under a mac and great coat on top of the bed.

As there were no games many boys went out to Spout Hills tobogganing every afternoon. There were not enough toboggans, though the workshops were hard at it producing more, so people slid down on surf boards, sheets of corrugated iron bent up in the front and so on. It was very dangerous, especially as there were bramble bushes and trees to avoid and a stream at the bottom. Boys wore corps uniform for this and corps boots. It should not have shaken us but the army uniform was the best made and toughest equipment we had. It was almost windproof and very good against thorns.

There was quite a lot of skating. Most skates were clamped skates fixed on to corps boots. Early in the term that notorious Headmaster's notice appeared on the School board: 'There will be no skating until water has been passed by me.' The School laughed like a drain!

In the autumn of 1949 over 200 relatives, friends and OGs gathered on the Chapel Lawn before the ceremony of the Unveiling and Dedication of the 1939–45 War Memorial. At least 650 Greshamians served in the forces and 107 died. Their names were inscribed on a tablet of Hopton Wood stone surmounted by the School crest in colour and gilt. Three high-ranking OGs representing the three Services performed the unveiling and Arthur Gamble preached the Sermon. As with many other public schools a great number of the early casualties were young men who rushed to join the RAF and died in the Battle of Britain or in bombing raids over Germany and occupied Europe. As in the First World War many decorations were won including three DSOs with bar. Of these the most colourful (and the most decorated) was Major-General G.P. 'Peter' Gregson who won an MC at Tobruk, his first DSO in Italy and his second after the Normandy landings. He was also awarded the *Croix de Guerre* and twice mentioned in despatches. Gregson finished the war a full Colonel and was Commander Royal Artillery in Korea where he travelled in a jeep with two New Zealand Maori signallers, a pair of shotguns and his faithful labrador, once returning from his rounds with seven brace of quail. The exploits of two other OGs are more widely known though their names are hardly remembered by any except those who served with them.

Tobogganing on the Spout Hills.

Philip Toosey won a DSO in the days leading up to the fall of Singapore, was captured and spent the war as Senior British Officer in several POW camps including that immortalised by the film *The Bridge on the River Kwai* when 'his' character was played by Alec Guinness. The truth was very far from that portrayed in the film but Toosey suffered beatings and solitary detention in his determination to secure humane treatment for the men under his command. He managed to maintain the self-respect and discipline of his fellow prisoners – Dutch, British and Australian – and was instrumental in the formulation of a scheme whereby money was obtained (at the risk of the death penalty) to obtain extra food and medicine for the sick. Toosey was further decorated with the CBE after the War and was later knighted for his work with the Far Eastern Prisoner of War Association and for his charitable work in connection with the School of Tropical Medicine in Liverpool. He had shown extraordinary humanity and forgiveness in saving one of his chief Japanese tormentors from the death penalty through his testimony before a War Crimes Tribunal.

Unveiling the memorial to those killed in the 1939–45 War (above).

The Memorial Tablet of Hopton Wood stone 1939–1945 (below).

Joe Baker-Cresswell was leading 3rd Escort Group guarding convoy OB318 out of Liverpool in the Atlantic in the destroyer 'Bulldog'. It was 9 May 1941 and the ability of U-boats to gather in packs through their Enigma cipher machines was causing disastrous damage to the Allied merchant fleets. The breaking of the code was crucial and engaged the full-time attention of the experts at Bletchley Park. The U110 had already sunk two merchant ships before its periscope was sighted and three escorts closed in dropping a pattern of depth charges. The U-boat was forced to the surface and many of the crew were rescued, though not the Captain, Julius Lamp. Baker-Cresswell saw an opportunity to board the submarine and ordered all prisoners below. 'Bulldog's' whaler made several trips as U110 was stripped of all equipment that could be moved, including an Enigma cipher machine with its settings for 9 May still intact, and priceless code-books which were snatched by the boarding commander Sub-Lt Balme. U110 was taken in tow but sank as the weather worsened. Bletchley Park officers could not believe their

The Headmaster and the
Country Life *trophy 1949.*

eyes when they were presented with two large packing cases of treasures. The code was broken though the Official Secrets Act prevented the story from emerging for many years. The incident had a major bearing on the battle of the Atlantic and it was no exaggeration when the King, while investing Baker-Cresswell with the DSO, remarked that the capture of U110 was perhaps the most important event in the whole war at sea. Baker-Cresswell died in 1997 at the age of 96 just before a television documentary series on the work of the code-breakers of Bletchley Park was released. The story was later told in a feature film, *Enigma.*

Despite the rapidly increasing numbers, academic standards remained consistent and by 1949 the Headmaster was regularly reporting an average of three or four Oxbridge awards, about the same as in the highly successful 1930s. One notable Girton Scholarship which Gresham's could not claim, but in which the School had a major investment, was that won by Camilla Crump in 1951. Camilla was one of the first of many Runton Hill girls who came over to attend science classes unavailable to them at their own School. Competition for Oxbridge places was growing as the grammar schools increasingly pointed their brightest towards the 'dreaming spires.' The rising roll did much for sport. Philip Newell had sanctioned the first inter-school matches in 1937 and now the fixture list grew to include most of the East Anglian public schools. In 1949 the Headmaster could announce that throughout the year only one first-team fixture against another school had been lost. He also waxed lyrical about the success of the shooting VIII who had lifted the *Country Life* trophy at Bisley that year. It was a sport in which Gresham's continued to shine. A number of Oxbridge 'Blues' were gained at this time particularly at hockey. Andrew Corran at Oxford and Peter Croft at Cambridge represented their Universities at cricket too. Croft went on to play hockey for England and was a member of the British Olympic Team in 1960 following in the footsteps of Dennis Eagan who won a bronze medal in 1956. Corran gained his County Cricket

Route March at CCF Camp
1949.

The Rugby Field in September.

cap for Nottinghamshire. Andrew Mulligan played Rugby for Cambridge, Ireland and the British Lions. His legendary team-mate, Tony O'Reilly, accompanied Mulligan back to Holt on several occasions to play against the School – golden moments vividly remembered by admiring spectators.

The Gresham reported continuing interest in a wide range of activities, especially Natural History, Debating and House and School Drama. The remarkable Gresham's grapevine enabled the editor to keep everyone informed of the progress of distinguished former pupils, the summer edition for 1951 quoting, for example, an article in *Vogue* magazine about the exploits of theatre director Peter Brook who had left the School in 1941:

> The *enfant terrible* of the theatre, still only 26, has become almost one of its Grand Old Men, so widely is his reputation known and revered. To three productions recently running in London – *The Little Hut*, the unlucky *A Penny For A Song* and the by now classic *Ring Around The Moon*, he will soon add *The Winter's Tale* with Gielgud, Wynyard and Flora Robson; scenery designed by Sophie Fedorovitch. Brook's work has matured away from tricks and 'for the hell of it' shocks to the beautiful, sensitive, always exciting brilliance of his *Measure for Measure* at Stratford last year.

Peter Brook was a late arrival at Gresham's, a loner, opinionated, sometimes abrasive, critical, brilliant. He maintains in his autobiography *Threads of Time* that the only teacher who enthused him in any way was Hoult Taylor, producer of plays, 'an exciting outsider who could be wickedly indiscreet. The greatest privi-

Andrew Mulligan in his British Lions Jersey: Auckland 1959.

Backstage, Theatre-in-the-Woods.

lege was to be invited by him to tea . . .' Nevertheless, Brook certainly became involved at School. He acted in two plays, debated precociously and regularly, and on his last Speech Day, at the age of 16, won no fewer than five prizes for English, French, German and Instrumental Music.

The re-opening of the Theatre-in-the-Woods coincided with the Jubilee of Howson's appointment to Gresham's and the following year Hoult Taylor direct- ed *A Midsummer Night's Dream* to celebrate the 50th anniversary of the first play set in the Waterloo belt before the 'new' School buildings along the Cromer Road were more than an architect's plans. The OG *Newsletter* for October 1951 includ- ed an article by an unnamed writer who had clear memories of being present at that first night half a century before:

> Just on half a century ago the School company of those days did that same piece (careful-
> ly Bowdlerised by G.W.S.H. himself) under a beech tree near the Baths and impressed on
> my youthful mind that Shakespeare-Trying-To-Be-Funny was the very nadir of tedium. Folks
> were more easily amused in those days, and no doubt the besotted cluckings of adoring
> parents and the laudatory notices in the local press (written of course by the producer) con-

cealed from us how closely we were adhering to the Greek dictum that a gentleman might learn to play the flute but not too well.

To be fair to the luckless producer of that day we must remember that apart from the pardonable ignorance of his job and apart from the ill-fitting wigs and frowsy costumes supplied by Messrs Israel, Isaac and Jacob in which the faint aura of a hundred predecessors battled not unsuccessfully against a powerful disinfectant, he had to neutralise the steady, dumb conviction of a resentful cast that they had been brought out there to make fools of themselves. Those were the days of the Strong, Silent Man and acting was the business of rogues, vagabonds and giggling girls. Shakespeare, moreover, was Education; a spawner of footnotes and all the drearier forms of exam-fodder. The more honour to him then (was it Langford-James?) that he succeeded in breaking down our inhibitions to some extent, so that the next production was better, and the next better still – though not, it seems, good enough to be included in the list on the programme. Geoffrey Shaw's delightful music and the building of the present Theatre gave us a better conceit of ourselves, and one likes to think that when the latter opened with *Twelfth Night* we were not so bad; but never did we get within measurable distance of what we saw on Saturday evening.

For here were *actors*: moving with assurance, making their lines alive, timing their business with the accuracy of old troupers – and all in flannels and blazers, with the very minimum of gear. From Bottom tearing a cat in his Ercles vein and Thisbe's inspired voice-production to the humblest super – and that is where good production shows – they carried such conviction that it was the first time I had realised what a set of ill-mannered, sniggering snobs the top-people of that day must have been. Can one imagine the squire's party at a performance of the Women's Institute behaving like Theseus and his gang? Even my long-established views on the Bore of Avon were shaken and I laughed out loud, twice.

It was worth putting that old Theatre to rights, wasn't it?

Academically the country saw a great change in the examination system when the School Certificate gave way to the General Certificate of Education – Ordinary and Advanced Levels. The Headmaster was able to report a smooth transition borne out by the statistics published in July 1952 and 1953. Four Open Awards at Oxbridge included one to John Tusa, later to become one of television's leading broadcasters and Managing Director of the Barbican Centre. Coronation Year (1953) was also marked by the production of the latest 'swept back' wing research aircraft designed by David Keith Lucas, the OG Chief Designer of Short Brothers, and the exploits of Tom Bourdillon. Together with his father, Bourdillon designed the lightweight oxygen equipment which ensured the success of the British Everest Expedition though he himself failed by just 400 feet to wrest the ultimate glory from Edmund Hillary and Sherpa Tenzing. Bourdillon followed in the footsteps of two earlier Gresham's men of Everest, Peter Lloyd in 1938 and Percy Wyn Harris who in 1933 reached a point only 1,000 feet from the summit and on the way up came upon the ice axe used by Mallory or Irvine in their fateful assault in 1924.

To illustrate the width of Greshamian ambition, the same edition that highlighted Bourdillon's achievement also noted the death of Robert Mawdesley who attained immortality as *The Archers*' first Walter Gabriel. And the summer of 1953 saw the retirement of one of the school's great characters, Tommy Birtles, who was in and out of the Yorkshire Cricket XI at a time when Holmes and Sutcliffe ruled the roost. After years of success in the Yorkshire Leagues in 1931 he came to Gresham's as Head Groundsman and Cricket Professional, and his humorous anecdotes of eccentric umpires, cup ties, cricketers, mankind and Yorkshire in particular were as memorable as his appearances for the Masters XI, his bowling in the nets and his coaching in the art of the straight bat.

A year later another 'institution' left Gresham's, to start a preparatory school near Stratford-on-Avon. For nineteen years, having succeeded J.R. Eccles, L.A.M. 'Max' Parsons was Housemaster of Woodlands ably assisted for much of that time by his mother and by his sister Barbara. He kept the flame of Latin alive in a School more dedicated to the sciences and for twenty-five years, mostly from a shooting stick, he produced some of the best schoolboy hockey sides in the country.

Martin Olivier was a complex character: he had managed the return from Newquay, he had begun to appoint some excellent staff, he knew every boy by name and showed great interest in their activities. He had, however, reintroduced corporal punishment, which was diametrically opposed to the tradition established by Eccles and Newell, and sport held a far more dominant position than had formerly been the case. The latter was, perhaps, inevitable and the former was partly due to the collapse of the honour system and partly was Olivier's response to the perceived (by some) relaxation of discipline during the Newquay years. Though he often showed great kindness and cared greatly for his boys he could show his emotional side in public and his unpredictability did not endear him. He was prone to critical outbursts and his temperament could be volatile. Perhaps significantly he gave in *Who's Who* as one of his major interests 'producing plays' and this he continued at Gresham's, notably in a staff production of *The Winslow Boy* in which he acted himself and shared the direction with Hoult Taylor and Malcolm Freegard. One of his most widely quoted sayings was 'Larry [Laurence Olivier, his cousin] may have the looks; I am the actor.'

So despite the promising position established since the return from Newquay, all was not well behind the scenes. By 1954 the staff appear to have become divided over their Headmaster. It was no secret that Max Parsons, who considered Woodlands to be very much his own little empire, and Martin Olivier detested one another. Various matters were brought to the Governors' attention by parents, and, importantly, by some senior pupils. Several extraordinary meetings of the Governors were held over the months following the end of the summer term 1954. There was much at stake, quite apart from the Headmaster's future and the School's reputation. 1955 was the quatercentenary of the School's foundation and plans for the celebrations were far advanced. It was a poisoned chalice for the newly appointed Chairman of Governors, Weston Backhouse, but after further deliberations it was announced that Martin Olivier would leave the School in April and that once again Bruce Douglas would hold the fort for the summer term until a new Headmaster took up office in September 1955. The decision caused considerable division in the staffroom and some bewilderment amongst those parents and pupils who saw only an apparently thriving and positive school.

In the Old Greshamian *Newsletter* for the summer term 1955 Charles Linnell, the School's historian, who had been appointed Chaplain in 1946 and had retained his abiding interest in the School after leaving for parish work in 1950, wrote what

must have been a very difficult 'vale' to the departing Headmaster. He compared Olivier with Henry Mazy who had become Headmaster in the wake of the English Civil War when Gresham's had undergone considerable stress. Both Mazy and Olivier had been called upon to re-establish the School following periods of extreme instability and both had achieved that aim. In the same issue there appeared a letter from Martin Olivier announcing that he had been appointed to be first Headmaster of Guthlaxton Grammar School, one of two new secondary schools in what became known as the 'Leicestershire experiment' which aimed to provide an alternative to the 11+ examination and anticipated the coming of the comprehensive system. Martin Olivier died suddenly in 1959 having impressed many by his energy and enthusiasm in his new challenge.

Speech Day 1949 in the restored Theatre-in-the-Woods.

In the steps of the Beatles: 'Highway Four' one of many Gresham's 1960s pop groups.

5

Four Centuries and a Quarter More:

LOGIE BRUCE LOCKHART 1955–1982

The Governors appointed as Martin Olivier's successor a 33-year-old with just seven years' teaching experience at Tonbridge. It may have seemed a long shot in view of the circumstances, but it worked – for twenty-seven years. Logie Bruce Lockhart, like Howson, came from a schoolmastering stable. He had been head boy at Sedbergh where his father was Headmaster and had gone straight to Sandhurst in 1942, before serving first with the Sherwood Foresters and then with the Household Cavalry, with whom at the end of the War he had been one of the first British soldiers to enter Belsen concentration camp. His career at Cambridge was remarkable: Choral studentship at St John's College, Scholarship and Wright Prize for Modern Languages, Larmar Award for all-round contribution to the College, and Blues for Rugby and Squash (with cheerful appearances for the Crusaders at cricket). He then won five Rugby caps for Scotland. He was a natural countryman with a lifelong love of fishing, and was an expert on fungi. He cultivated his knowledge of ornithology in company with Dick Bagnall-Oakeley and was a more-than-competent water-colourist. He was something of an authority on the music of Schubert, a great raconteur and an entertaining public speaker. He also wrote articles on a wide range of topics in newspapers and periodicals. His views were forthright and he was a self-proclaimed scourge of reds-under-the-bed. His support for independent education was uncompromising, leading to occasional utterances in public which might have been better left unsaid. But in all things he was encouraging: he championed the individualist and the unorthodox amongst staff and pupils. Above all, he was profoundly humane.

Logie Bruce Lockhart, Headmaster (1955–1982) c.1970.

He was a man to put his School on the map and within three weeks of his headmastership he had to play host to the Duke of Edinburgh on his visit to celebrate the 400th anniversary of Gresham's Foundation. It was not Prince Philip's first or last visit. He had played hockey for Gordonstoun in 1938, was later to open the Girls' House named after him, and returned to do the honours in 1998 when the Auden Theatre was unveiled.

Academic standards at Gresham's had always been high at the top end. This did not change and the sciences continued to produce open scholars of real calibre, as typified by the Partington brothers, all three of whom won Open Scholarships

James Dyson running in the School Cross Country 1964.

Staff 1959.

*Mr Fairchild – the last
School Porter (retired 1965).*

to Oxford, and by Ian Powrie whose brilliant success at Cambridge made his death in the Korean Airlines disaster in 1983 the more poignant. The School's reputation for producing independent and creative alumni was enhanced by the later careers of Stephen Frears – the award-winning film director – and James Dyson, whose early frustrations in attempting to find financial backing in Britain for his inventions ended when he went it alone and created an empire on the back of his bagless vacuum cleaner. Dyson returned to Gresham's several times to inspire others with his story and readily acknowledged his debt to the School and its Headmaster in giving him financial support to continue his education following the early death of his father whilst he was still at Holt.

Logie Bruce Lockhart instinctively followed some of Howson's liberal aspirations, though he was anything but a liberal in his introduction of the Corphaena award deliberately setting out to celebrate distinction in any area of school life. Its unashamedly elitist nature might have met with the great refounder's disapproval, but it made clear that excellence on the games field should be equated with excellence in any other sphere from music or drama to archaeology, public speaking or, of course, academic achievement. Those who were genuinely without the sporting talent or interest found that they could be released from compulsory games, provided that they could find alternative employment such as forestry, school work, social service or music practice. The Combined Cadet Force (CCF) flourished and was one of the first contingents in the 1960s to organise 'greenfield' summer camps in Wales, Scotland and the Peak District at a time when attachment to army or air-force stations, marching and mock battles were still the norm. In one of these pioneering ventures the author's link with Wellington College (where he had completed his teaching practice during his PGCE) saved the day for the RAF camp in Snowdonia. It had rained continuously for three days and the 'amateur' shelters brought along by the cadets were no match for the Welsh monsoons. Wellington College took pity and offered the use of a couple of 160-pounder tents. The lesson was learned the hard way but it was never forgotten. From an early stage the value of the Duke of Edinburgh's Award Scheme was realised and climbing expeditions in Great Britain, Europe and the Atlas Mountains attracted increasing numbers of boys and, later, girls.

Shooting, first under Dick Bagnall-Oakeley, John Mainstone and then John Rowley, put the name of Gresham's firmly on the national and international map with regular selections for the Athelings National Schools Team. Squash, under the inspiration of Malcolm Willstrop, whose coaching skills gained praise from the great Jonah Barrington, swept all before it and produced a number of players of national standard, the best known being the British champion and world number four, Gawain Briars. Sailing was another success and a popular 'minor' sport with Ken Hervé becoming World Champion in the Hornet and Flying Dutchman classes. Rugby, hockey and cricket remained the 'major' games and in the Bruce Lockhart period the School's reputation grew considerably. Large numbers represented the county and some went further. Nick Youngs played scrum-half for England and acknowledged his debt to Tony Cuff's coaching in the process, whilst at Hockey Richard Leman eventually won over a hundred England caps and represented Britain at two Olympics, winning a Bronze and then a Gold Medal. Paul Searle-Barnes, Richard Hands, Andrew Marlow and the composer Roderick Watkins were just four who pursued their musical talents in the professional world, as did Stephen Bentley-Klein and George Stiles in the more commercial and pop-

Tony Cuff.

John Rowley (standing extreme left) watches Nick Tricker (nearest camera) at the 1,000-yard firing point.

The Open Air Theatre, 1970.

Graeme Fife directs the summer play.

ular field. Nigel Dick and William Osborne both made names for themselves in the American movie business, Nigel as a director (in particular of music videos for which he won a Lifetime Achievement Award) and William as a screenwriter, whilst back in the UK Julian Jarrold, escaping from the family business in Norwich, steadily made his mark as a TV director. On the literary scene several OGs made their mark. John Lanchester won the Whitbread Prize for his first novel *The Debt to Pleasure*, also picking up the Betty Trask and the Hawthornden Awards.

School plays were still performed in the Open Air Theatre though regular Shakespeare productions became things of the past. However, full-length plays were produced each year by every House, providing an important social and communal function as well as introducing generations of boys and girls to the whole theatrical experience. The standard of these productions was high and performances of musicals such as *Oh What a Lovely War* and *Guys and Dolls* competed for billboard space with comedies, Whitehall farces and classics including *Journey's End* and *Waiting for Godot*. The dual use of the Dining Hall gave far greater scope to producers and directors constrained by the cramped staging in Houses. Debating continued to thrive and the traditional Exhibitions Day preceding the end-of-year prize-giving demonstrated the strength and breadth of societies and activities of all kinds.

The late 1960s and early 1970s saw the rise of student unrest fuelled by CND and the anti-Vietnam War movement. Many will recall the national and international demonstrations, most vividly the young students of Paris marching arm in arm with strikers down the Champs Élysées, the occupation of the London School of Economics, and the bloodshed on the campuses of American universities. Throughout the UK, schools, especially those with sixth forms, were rocked by pupil subversion and the clamour for change. Probably Logie Bruce Lockhart was right in saying that Norfolk's geographical position insulated it from the worst of the disorder. He acknowledged the underlying idealism whilst deploring publicly the 'vicious and destructive criticism' of magazines such as *Oz* and *Black Dwarf* and the teachings of the *Little Red School Book*. He also attacked the 'cult of shabbiness in manners, morals and appearances.' Certainly much time was taken up with discussions on length of hair and width of trouser bottoms and there was a strong feeling of disaffection and disillusion amongst sections of the School. The decision to sanction changes in uniform for those in the Sixth Form was part of the approach adopted, which was prepared to discuss and implement change whilst holding firm to those principles which were fundamental to the School's ethos. Following the American example, and along with many other independent schools, Gresham's introduced a School Council in June 1969 with its members elected by the boys, which gave direct access to the Headmaster. It met regularly and a summary of its conclusions was readily available to all – a welcome early example of 'glasnost'.

M.J. Crossley Evans on his way to Sunday Chapel.

The first meeting was met with apathy, understandable suspicion and even open contempt, but the editorial in *The Gresham* for March 1970 considering the effectiveness of the Council at the end of its first year, acknowledged the seriousness with which the authorities had considered all twenty-six innovations and modifications suggested – over half of which were implemented and only four of which were rejected outright. The majority of the sceptics were won over and the editorial commended 'the active support and interest of the community' which led to the conclusion that the experiment was, thus far at least, a success.

One major problem in all boarding schools at the time was that of compulsory Chapel. There was a clear decline in religious faith within the country, especially amongst the youth, and the atmosphere on Sunday mornings or evenings in Chapel was uneasy. Some pupils defied convention by refusing to bow their heads

Debating Society in Big School 1979: Andrew Ferris provokes his opponents. Mr Michael Barrett presides.

for prayers and would not say the Creed, nor turn to the altar. Singing was poor, though there was little orchestrated silence. The Headmaster maintained credibility and integrity by countering requests for absence on conscientious grounds with a reasonable demand for an academic and cogent written argument, giving reasons and revealing a knowledge of the spiritual issues involved. No one took up the challenge.

Gresham's was fortunate to ride out these turbulent years, which created real strife in some schools, in relative calm. The tolerance and patience of the Headmaster, whose homilies in Assembly came from sources as various as the Buddha, Mohammed, Jung, the German philosophers, Billy Graham and Confucius, was a factor certainly. Perhaps the long tradition of good communication between pupils and assistant teaching staff, particularly the increasing number of younger appointees in this period, allowed genuinely held grievances to be expressed. Some good came of it all, but it was an uncomfortable time.

Ever since the return from Newquay, the all-male regiments of Gresham's had been infiltrated by small groups of young ladies from Runton Hill, which school could not provide the necessary facilities for its science Sixth Formers. In 1971, the first two direct-entry day girls were accepted as Gresham's pupils for their A Levels. As pioneers and excellent academics and contributors, as well as persons of considerable fortitude, their names deserve mention – Rhona Slator and Vicky Holliday. Both had brothers at Gresham's and both went on to become doctors. In 1972 five more girls were accepted into the Sixth Form and the experiment

Sixth Form Study in Oakeley: Sarah Cordeaux in residence.

Notice Boards in Big School corridor.

gained a momentum of its own. There was no conscious decision-making about co-education at this stage, though the Headmaster was certainly sympathetic to the concept. Staff sons were educated free but there was nothing on offer for staff daughters, and demand was strengthened by the wishes of parents who wanted their children at the same school. Gradually more girls entered the Sixth Form and, of the first twenty, nineteen gained University places and five open awards were won. Not everyone welcomed the change. Some staff were strongly opposed though the majority were in favour. At first, facilities for girls were makeshift and unsatisfactory and by 1978 it was clearly time to organise things on a more formal basis. John and Jenny Rayner were appointed Housemaster and Housemistress of Oakeley House, named after Dick Bagnall-Oakeley who had recently died within months of his retirement from the staff. It was based in the cramped, and not easily adapted, Old Sanatorium built opposite Howson's in 1903. Its architectural style was described by Rayner as 'Gresham's dacha'. The 'new' Sanatorium site had been rejected because it was considered insecure, bordering, as it did, woodland on the far and remote eastern limits of the School estate. There is an irony in the fact that twenty-five years later the third Girls' House, Britten, moved into these very premises.

It was not an easy beginning but Gresham's had many advantages. There were few alternative independent schools for local parents to choose from, and as numbers grew and boarding for girls became viable, parents seeking co-education for their children rose too. The influence of the 1960s may have been partially responsible for changing views, and Gresham's was early into the market, therefore

Tallis.

attracting excellent girl candidates from whom the best could be selected. Music and drama benefited of course, and there were those who saw the female presence, rather patronisingly, as 'civilising'. There were certainly cultural and social advantages for all despite the perceived dangers of the integration of the sexes – the dilemma the Headmaster presented as 'barbed wire and machine guns or prayer and the pill.'

When Logie Bruce Lockhart was Chairman of HMC Eastern Division, he broke new ground by inviting the headmistresses of GSA (the Girls' Schools Association) to a joint meeting. They tore into the unsuspecting male delegates. Headmasters, they said, were stealing girls from GSA, sacrificing them to the attempt to civilise the louts of HMC schools. Half the tiny minority of girls would have their heads turned; half would have their self-esteem crushed by lack of attention. There were no female role models in boys' school staff rooms, there had been no proper training of male staff, the schools were simply unprepared to receive girls, who would be shouted down by the boys in class so that their results would suffer. It all needed saying and there was much in what the headmistresses said and felt. There were lessons to be learnt but there would be no turning back. There is no doubt that this fresh Sixth Form infusion (which soon included boys as well as girls and the first of those on Assisted Places) was hugely beneficial and stimulating for all. Oakeley was soon performing, in the eyes of some boys and staff, all too well in the House Music Competition, one of the highlights of the School calendar. House play producers welcomed the chance to cast 'real' girls instead of embarrassed boys with size-11 feet. But this was still a one-sided advantage: girls being of value to a boys' school. The Rayners fought a number of battles for the girls whilst the slow educational process towards co-education unfolded. Perhaps the turning point came in 1979 (the year after the official opening of Oakeley) when John Rayner directed the first girls' House play in Big School, *The Prime of Miss Jean Brodie*. Those boys who came to ogle or scoff were quickly awed by the performances of such as Helen Shaftoe and Hannah Ramuz. It was a defining moment. By the time other boys' schools were feeling the pinch and scrambling to tap into the girl market in the late 1980s and early 1990s, Gresham's had opened a second Girls' House and was contemplating a third.

Logie Bruce Lockhart was a brilliant public speaker, as he revealed every year at Speech Day. He told good stories against himself: slightly uncomfortable after showing crisply attired foreign parents around the ground floor of Howson's on a bad day, he asked whether they would like to continue the tour upstairs. 'No need, Headmaster,' came the reply, 'I do not send my son here to be comfortable, I send him to sleep in filthy English dormitory'; or the day he showed a slightly disorganised-looking couple round and was about to say goodbye amongst the cars on the Parade Ground, when he decided there was just time to nip down to see the Junior School. He held the car door open, the father got in with his wife beside him, and L.B.L. sat in the back. After a quick tour round Kenwyn, he again held open the car door. The father hesitated. 'Don't you like driving, Mr Bruce Lockhart?' he asked. 'Yes, as a matter of fact I do,' L.B.L. replied. 'Why do you ask?' 'Well – why don't you drive your own car?' There was a pause. 'It isn't my car.' And it wasn't the parents' either. A certain absentmindedness – studied or real – became something of a legend in the Common Room. There was the famous occasion when L.B.L. was discussing the new School year which was about to begin, with his Second Master and two senior colleagues. Gazing out of his study window overlooking the Parade Ground, he spied an unfamiliar figure carrying a pile of books towards Big School. 'Who's that?' he asked. 'That's the new Languages teacher.' 'Oh God!' came the appalled response, 'I've appointed the wrong man.' A story sent in by an OG illustrates L.B.L.'s sang-froid and his psychological mastery. Tallis, unsurprisingly, became a regular feature of the prospective parents' tour and it was the Headmaster's habit to raise his voice several decibels on entering the House, perhaps to announce his imminent arrival to unstudious inmates. On this occasion, the Head of House and another senior were enjoying a musical coffee interlude and it was not until the visitors were already in the corridor that realisation struck the pair. The owner of the study flicked off the music and buried his head in his book. The Head of House lost his nerve and dived into the built-in wardrobe. In strode L.B.L.. 'This is Rupert _____, who is applying to Cambridge this year' (which was news to Rupert). 'You can see how light and spacious it is,' continued the Headmaster, indicating various features. 'They have spacious cupboards too,' he boomed, opening the door to reveal the crouching figure of the other boy. Without a pause he continued, 'And this is Richard ____, Head of House.' For several days two very nervous young men awaited the call to the Headmaster's study. It never came.

The Central Feeding Block.

*Geoffrey Winterbone
('Smokey Joe') deals with a
coal delivery at Farfield in
1975 (above).*

*New Kenwyn's 'square
cupola set diagonally'
(below).*

Over thirty years on, the author recalls a visit to the Headmaster in his ridiculously placed study in a garret at the top of Big School above the Staff Common Room. It was soon after the end of the Summer Term and the Head was about to decamp to more suitable and palatial quarters in the new Dining Hall block. Entering the room the relatively new assistant master was confronted by an empty room save for a desk at which the Secretary sat taking dictation. Logie Bruce Lockhart himself reclined, firmly wedged, legs in the air, in the only other piece of office equipment, an enormous wicker waste-paper basket. Clad in shorts and his Cambridge rugby sweater the Headmaster looked up, smiled and said, 'Hello, Steve. All ears.' Both he and his excellent assistant, inured to such eccentricities, appeared totally unaware of the extraordinary prospect presented.

In a period of over a quarter of a century, it is not surprising that the architectural landscape of the School altered greatly. The quatercentennial appeal in 1955 provided the Music School and Biology laboratories constructed, not entirely successfully, to blend with the napped flint of the adjacent Chapel. Numbers had reached 350 which by now included 93 junior boys living in overcrowded conditions in Kenwyn. It was clear that something significant would have to be done. Thus in 1958 'New' Kenwyn was built on the vacant plot over the Cromer Road and alongside Crossways. 'New' Kenwyn was a masterly construction. Designed by Grenfell Baines with plenty of light and space, it attracted the notice of Sir Nikolaus Pevsner in his 1962 *Buildings of England* series. 'Pretty' was Pevsner's description, 'of pale brick with a square cupola set diagonally.' In 1963 the opening of Tallis provided a very modern senior boarding house which at one time had been conceived as special accommodation for boys in their final A Level year, so that they might be prepared for University life ahead. In the end, it emerged as a fifth boarding house for the rapidly expanding numbers of those seeking entry to public schools, the result of the post-war baby boom and the Macmillan slogan

*Crossways Common Room:
The Junior School, 1970s.*

Duncan Bruce Lockhart makes a break.

'you've never had it so good.' Tallis was named after a Gresham's Headmaster of the seventeenth century who had revitalised the School at a time when it had been in steep decline. John and Margaret Coleridge, who were ideally suited to the task of launching Gresham's' 1960s flagship, moved in. Between 1966 and 1976 bed-sitters for Sixth Formers were created by converting studies and dormitories and in Howson's by building an extension. An appeal to parents and OGs (heavily underwritten by the Fishmongers' Company) produced the Reith Laboratories opened by the great man in 1969, including a fine Lecture Theatre and more space for Physics and Chemistry. In 1970 came a major change – central feeding – and the construction of a large flat-roofed building on the extreme edge of the Parade Ground bordering the Cromer Road. This facility also included a Sanatorium, a large staff Common Room and dining area and, most importantly, it brought together the offices of the Bursar and Headmaster which hitherto had been positioned on opposite sides of the Cromer Road. Failure to decide upon a suitable name for the construction led to its dismal christening as the CFB or Central Feeding Block. Another appeal prepared the way for the indoor swimming pool (1976) and also for important extensions and renovations to the Junior School. The creation of Oakeley in 1978 brought to an end the major development programme of the Bruce Lockhart years though an appeal for the building of a Sports Hall was reaching its successful climax at the time of his retirement in 1982.

John Coleridge in relaxed retirement. 'J.K.C.' was Acting Headmaster for a term before Hugh Wright arrived.

Much of this building programme had been carried out during the sixteen-year Bursarship of John Purdy. Purdy had been a distinguished colonial administrator who had spent many years in Nigeria rising to become Senior Resident in Kano Province. He was used to command as was L.B.L. who, in his tribute to Purdy at the latter's funeral in 1999, admitted, 'There is usually and necessarily a tricky relationship between Heads and Bursars.' But they got on well much to the advantage of Gresham's. It was about ten years into their alliance that Purdy remarked, 'You know, Logie, my job is really just the same as it was in Kano [Nigeria]: I look after the eccentric Emir's lavatories, surrounded by turbulent natives [perhaps a refer-

John Purdy, Bursar.

ence to Housemasters and their wives] and confused by directions from an out-of-touch government in the capital.' In fact he quickly earned the trust of the Fishmongers' Company and did much to re-establish closer links with Fishmongers' Hall, greatly assisted by the long-serving and supportive Clerk to the Company (and to the Governors) Eric Earl.

The success of any school at any time depends to a large extent on the quality and character of its teachers. The 1960s and 1970s saw the appointment of many young staff and the birth of a large brood of staff children whose subsidised schooling caused successive Bursars an increasing financial headache. Staff parties and play productions (*Ring Around the Moon, Harlequinade*) strengthened the bonds of friendship and the staff Cricket XI provided an endless source of fisherman's tales including the fabled game at Wighton when local umpires in mackintoshes ignored the ever more desperate appeals of the champions of Gresham's Common Room to manufacture a ten-wicket victory for the home side – and then comprehensively destroyed the demoralised staff team at darts. Wighton Church Tower collapsed early the following week, the foundations laid 600 years before finally shaken perhaps by the seismographic stumping attempts of the staff wicket-keeper. Gresham's was generally a happy Common Room in the Bruce Lockhart era, and north Norfolk is a seductive place to live. It is hardly surprising, then, that there were many long-serving staff members, all in their various ways and according to their talents, contributing towards the overall success of the School in this period.

The 'old guard' of pre-war appointees included Bernard Sankey who succeeded Bruce Douglas as Second Master in 1963, and Paul Colombé, scholarly mathematician and wartime naval officer in Russian convoys who took over the role on Sankey's retirement. Both had been Housemasters, of Farfield and Old School

Stuart Webster teaches the art of the lino-cut.

House respectively. John Williams was another who spent a brief period at Newquay before becoming a Commando in the Madagascar campaign. Rugby coach (and one of the founders of Holt Rugby Club), Head of PE and Commander of the CCF, Williams' greatest work came in building up the strength and reputation of Kenwyn, later to become the Preparatory School. He was also the kindest of men, opening his home to many boys whose parents worked abroad in days when travel was far from easy. Stuart Webster arrived with the return from Cornwall. A diminutive Art teacher with twinkling eyes, a whooping laugh and a fund of stories (who can forget the Accrington Stanley Brass Band?), he would swing his legs in the White Lion and at other moments introduce himself thus: 'My name is Stuart Webster and I am standing up.' John Coleridge, another naval man, became Head of English and first Housemaster of Tallis before being appointed Second Master. A great promoter of the arts at Gresham's, a keen producer of plays for pupils and staff and always interested and encouraging, Coleridge ended his career as Acting Headmaster before the arrival of Hugh Wright in 1985. Bill Thomas was a Classicist and sportsman who made many runs for Norfolk whilst also coaching the school XI. He had the priceless knack of making games fun and was a great giggler and pipe-smoker. He was also successful Housemaster of Farfield before becoming the school's first Director of Studies having learned (and applied) a sense of proportion fighting the Japanese in the jungle before being wounded 'on the road to Mandalay.'

'Jumbo' Burrough in the School woods.

'Jumbo' Burrough, remembered by generations who learned craft and engineering drawing in his Department and who gained much knowledge of conservation by working with him in the school woods, had been captured in Greece and a POW in Germany. He was multi-talented as a musician and actor and was for many years at the heart of Common Room social life, as was Laurie Taylor who taught the juniors and joined the staff at Newquay. Another staff character was Rob Corbett, a craftsman who had been a pupil during the War and joined Jumbo to teach craft skills. Rob found out just how many friends he had when his Corpusty workshop burned down and was rebuilt with the aid of a hefty donation from OGs and colleagues.

Wilfred Andrews was briefly school Chaplain before the appointment of that supreme games player and hockey and tennis coach, Douglas Argyle, whose encyclopaedic knowledge of every public school in the land was legendary. Andrews became Housemaster of Woodlands and Head of History. A shy man, who was not always understood by the more extrovert of his pupils and House charges, his wit was much appreciated by those who knew him well and he could happily have been an Oxford don transported back to the eighteenth century. One of Andrews' greatest friends was Dick Bagnall-Oakeley who spent almost his entire life connected with Gresham's as pupil and teacher. Head boy, brilliant sportsman (he played hockey for Norfolk and gained his Shooting Blue at Cambridge), he was above all a lover of Norfolk, his native county. His talents as a naturalist, photographer, water-colourist, writer, broadcaster and raconteur with a mastery of Norfolk dialect found expression and an audience everywhere he went. Small

Bill Thomas, enthralled, watching golf.

Dick Bagnall-Oakeley.

wonder that so many pupils remember him with affection and awe. They learned far more from him than Geography O or A level. Indeed as an examination teacher he was not uniformly successful. But he was an educator second to none and a life-enhancer never to be forgotten.

Ron Coleman, who was also Housemaster of Farfield, succeeded Dick as Head of Geography assisted by John Walton. Walton, or 'Chop' as he was (and is) known, is best remembered as the builder of the school's high reputation in the Duke of Edinburgh Award Scheme with literally hundreds of Gold-standard candidates over the years. A climber and pot-holer he was for some years a formidable resident House Tutor in Woodlands. Another long-serving House Tutor was Michael Barrett (in Tallis) who later became Head of History. Like John Coleridge and John Rayner, Michael did much to encourage and promote the cultural life of the school in many ways. He was President of the Debating Society bringing a number of his friends to speak and to provide rich entertainment. He produced House Plays for many years and founded several societies connected with wine-tasting, the writings of Tolkien, the reconstruction of historic events (like the Duchess of Richmond's Ball before Waterloo) and most successfully of all, organising local excavations with his Archaeological Society. He wrote a book about school matrons and took a two-term sabbatical visiting Anglican Cathedrals throughout the former British Empire. Barrett's battles with severe illness in the years before his early retirement bring back memories of Dan Frampton. Joining the staff just after the War (he had fought in Italy and Palestine), Frampton taught mainly in the Junior School but coached the Hockey XI for a number of years and took over command of the CCF from John Williams. Both received the OBE for

A Biology practical: Mr Oliver Barnes unconvinced by Chris Nash (or vice versa).

108

Peter Corran teaching in 1958.

their services to the Cadet Corps. Dan Frampton fought cancer with great courage for over ten years.

Peter Corran, who joined the school in Newquay as a 13-year-old in 1944, won a major Oxford scholarship in Chemistry and returned to teach at Gresham's on Jan Day's departure. He built up the Chemistry Department, was Housemaster at OSH and made his greatest contribution as Director of Studies under Hugh Wright. A fine athlete who ran for Oxford, he was also a hockey coach of real distinction with an unbroken record of success over more than twenty-five years with the Under-15s. Another distinguished academic was Ron Cox whose Physics Department achieved respect and great success largely due to his tireless dedication. A master of English prose with a more than useful bass voice, Ron's contributions to Gresham's life were many and varied and included the study of Navigation (he had served in the Navy) and the running of the Sailing Club. Graham Smithers was another who made his mark primarily (but not exclusively!) on the academic side. A brilliant Mathematician, he took the Department to a dominant position in the school on occasions with over half the Sixth Form studying his subject. Occasionally a maverick in his views and actions, his success was legendary as was his expertise as Master of the Timetable. A fine 'pop' pianist, a man of great humanity and a keeper of birds, donkeys and dogs at his High Kelling home, Smithers can still be seen every Monday morning riding his bicycle into

Archaeological Society: Jonah Mitchell and board.

Synchronised hockey.

Steve Benson seeks the spot-light.

Holt to do his shopping before morning break.

The Biology Department has been fortunate in its distinguished trio who were appointed by Logie Bruce Lockhart: Oliver Barnes, Dave Horsley and Tony Leech (with an honourable mention for a fine teacher whose stay was much shorter, Grahame Lynn). All three have done much more than just teach their subject. All are naturalists of one kind or another in the Bagnall-Oakeley tradition. Barnes coached rugby and did much to return the Holt Lowes to its former glory; Horsley's expertise as an ornithologist enthused many pupils for whom he organised expeditions; Tony Leech revitalised the Natural History Society, worked hard to establish the Holt Country Park and has been the unofficial but extremely skilful school photographer for many years.

John Rayner's work in Oakeley has already been mentioned. His English teaching and play productions allied to his editorship of the *Old Greshamian Newsletter* and his work in promoting the school have been major contributions. Dick Copas' yeoman service as teacher and Head of Chemistry, master in charge of two major sports, organiser of ski-trips and expeditions, Housemaster of Howsons, Commander of the CCF and, finally, for sixteen years Second Master, have been referred to elsewhere. No one of L.B.L.'s appointments deserves greater praise than he.

The list goes on: Michael Allard, peerless organist, David Harris, companionable Choirmaster and accompanist, Keith Ashby, linguist, sailor, athlete and keeper of the CCF Motor Pool; Graham Worrall, Rugby coach and Housemaster of Farfield; Michael Hughes and Neville Jones who both led the fortunes of the Junior School before handing on their legacy to Tony Cuff; Richard Peaver, modern linguist, expert pianist and conductor, first Housemaster of Edinburgh and, following Dick Copas, Commander of the CCF. And finally two Heads of History, Masters in

House Tutors. From left, Richard Peaver, Martin Crossley Evans, Michael Barrett and Mike Runnals chair and cheer John Walton into matrimony.

charge of hockey and Housemasters (one of Woodlands and one of Tallis) who both went on to Headship (respectively at Bishop's Stortford College and at Clayesmore): Steve Benson and David Beeby.

For most of the Bruce Lockhart era, the School was fortunate to call on the services of a trio of remarkable laboratory assistants: Harold Cooke, a stalwart of St John's Ambulance, who learned his skills as a POW of the Japanese in Changi and who was awarded the BEM for his services to Physics at Gresham's; Arthur Lewis, who started as a groundsman in 1955 and then earned himself the necessary qualifications, through day-release, to become an outstanding Chemistry technician serving that Department for many years as well as being a notable footballer and cricketer in the locality; and David Olby, a great driving force in the Biology Department, who later became Domestic Manager and the creator of Dave's Diner.

Any considered assessment of Logie Bruce Lockhart's Headmastership must await a future School history, when time will allow a truer perspective. He did not forget the stark and sometimes brutal regime of his schooldays and he appreciated the space and privacy given to pupils when he arrived at Gresham's. He was also somewhat 'shocked' at the School's 'softness'. He set out to cast the net of opportunity as wide as possible in order to bring out latent or obvious talent in every boy and, later, girl. This meant encouraging activities, a wide range of minor sports, a broader choice of Sixth-Form subjects, opening up a country school to lectures and visits by international luminaries, from business and from the world of letters. Academically, a handful of open scholarships were won regularly at Oxford and Cambridge and other universities. Natural Sciences and Engineering still led the field, though History provided its fair share of Honours. Sport became much more competitive and standards rose, though excellence in all facets of school life was given equal value. Corporal punishment, though never excessive,

Hugh ('Pop') Mullens, an influential part-time English and classics teacher, immersed in Dickens.

Jonathan Morgan-Hughes and Mark Stutely settle a point of honour at dawn on the chapel lawn.

Mr Tony Cuff is 'gunged' for charity.

was regularly used as a part of the disciplinary code until the arrival of co-educa-tion put an end to this in the 1970s. There were some areas of academic life which were less successful than others and the coming of central feeding was a mixed blessing since it meant less emphasis on House identity. But the School expand-ed greatly and new facilities greatly enhanced the quality and disparity of life. The School was very different from the one visited by the Duke of Edinburgh for the quatercentenary celebrations in 1955. In 1981, the total numbers had risen to 578 (from 350) with 69 girls in Oakeley and 154 juniors in the two Houses, Crossways and Kenwyn. Day pupils had increased but the vast majority of senior boys, 80 per cent in fact, were still full boarders. The introduction of co-education must be seen as one of Bruce Lockhart's greatest successes and in this area Gresham's was, once again, well ahead of the field. Appointments to the staff showed a balance of all-rounders and high-calibre specialists, academic or sporting with a sprinkling of the talented unorthodox, like Graeme Fife and Duncan Hill. L.B.L. had his eccentricities and his deficiencies in administration, he did not relish unpopular or difficult decisions and would always find a compromise if he could, not pleasing everyone in doing so, but he led a united staff and presided over a generally happy school. Its reputation grew nationally during his time and much of this was due to his benign but powerful personality. He trusted and supported his staff, believed in and respected his pupils, and encouraged the whole community.

L.B.L.'s Speech Day addresses have been mentioned before. They always includ-ed trenchant comment on political, social or educational issues of the day, heart-lifting praise for pupils and staff in their achievements and rich pickings for the notebooks of those who came for his stories. Even when these reappeared, as in so long a reign they were bound to do, they caused hilarity amongst all ages gath-ered in the Theatre in the Woods to hear him. Not many slipped away early while he was on his feet. As an example of his oratory and his commitment to independent education, his ringing words at his last Speech Day will do well. He talked of the difficult years ahead (this was 1982) and the likelihood (not realised) of a change of government which, together with the recession of the time, would put greater pressure than ever on private schools:

> And when the fight is on, for Pete's sake don't let's apologise for ourselves like my distinguished colleagues in search of Liberal peerages: or make out shilly-shallying cases for compromise; or waffle on about the case against us in order to appear to be fair-minded. Make a stand on human rights, slap our achievements on the table, rely on our vast majority support [the polls then revealed that 75 per cent of the country supported the continued existence of private education], don't pretend to want to be anything but different to, or better than, state schools. If we don't why on earth should anyone bother to pay for us?
>
> And don't be afraid of change – after twenty-seven years of me it's overdue – fight to your last breath to ensure that in every possible way we are worth the great sacrifice that our parents are called upon to make. And survive you will deserve to, and survive you will.

End of an era: Logie Bruce Lockhart at work in his final year.

Jo and Logie Bruce Lockhart depart in style.

Second Formers.

6

Towards the Millennium:

1982–2002

It was never going to be easy for Logie Bruce Lockhart's successor. Although he had always allowed staff to get on with their jobs with the minimum of interference, delegation and clear demarcation were not his style; his was a benevolent despotism. It would require a highly experienced hand to guide Gresham's through the immediate post-Lockhart years. Tim Woods had a formidable CV. He was a South African who had won a Rhodes Scholarship to Oxford University where he had taken a D.Phil. in History and won a Double Blue in Squash and Hockey. He knew Gresham's well from his time at Felsted where he had coached sports teams which played many times at Holt. Tim's wife, Erica, was a great asset and a fine teacher and she and Tim proved excellent and inexhaustible hosts. What was lacking was real experience of management. Woods tackled a number of administrative and academic topics. He saw early on the need for a second girls' house and he created the post of Director of Studies. However, some appointments proved controversial and a certain failure in communication precipitated the crisis which resulted in Tim Woods' contract ending at Easter 1985. The dignity and courage he showed during his last two terms, as he worked out his notice, earned the respect of all and he moved on to a post at Trent College where his talents found full expression.

There was no doubting the experience of the next Headmaster. Hugh Wright had been educated at Kingswood, Bath, and had moved via Brentwood and Cheltenham, where he was a Housemaster, to become Headmaster of Stockport Grammar School. There he oversaw the doubling of the school's size and the establishing of full co-education. Whilst completing the year at Stockport he visited Holt on many occasions during John Coleridge's Acting Headship to discuss plans for change and development which could be implemented without delay when he took up office. An experienced manager, Hugh Wright provided the safe hands required at a School which, for all its apparent serenity, needed restored confidence within and without as well as administrative reform.

At the end of any long regime, change is inevitable and there was now a considerable urgency. In the words of John Smart, the Senior Editor of *The Gresham*, 'Hugh Wright found a growing school with a structure suitable to a smaller one.'

Dr Tim Woods.

Hugh Wright.

RSM John Bates, BEM, outstanding CCF School Staff Instructor 1973–1998.

On Bill Thomas' retirement Peter Corran came into his own as Director of Studies. Another key member of Wright's senior management team was John Russell who had succeeded John Purdy as Bursar towards the end of the Bruce Lockhart era. Russell's previous career as a naval purser served him well. He looked urgently at fee and pay structures, maintenance expenditure and the centralising of budgeting. His style was not always popular but he had creative ideas and he worked well with the Headmaster and the Governors. He had already overseen the construction of the sports hall, now the boarding houses received much needed attention; new English classrooms were built allowing departmental restructuring to take place, and Science and Language facilities were improved. Home Economics was introduced at A Level and, at the end of Wright's time, Theatre Studies too, taking advantage of the Studio created in the Thatched Buildings or 'Scruff Shacks' by Tim Brierley, Gresham's first Drama Director. Computing was widened and further space found for this and for Electronics within the Cairns Centre named after Rear Admiral the Earl Cairns, a former Chairman of Governors, opened in 1990 and funded by a successful appeal which provided an Art School and modern facilities to cope with the increasing demands of Design Technology. The Ministry of Defence funded a new indoor Shooting Range, a tribute to the excellence of the School's Combined Cadet Force and to the reputation of the small- and full-bore shooting teams and their coaches. Perhaps the most crucial decision (though with Oakeley numbers nearing a hundred by now a necessity) was the building of Edinburgh House. With boarding numbers falling nationally such an expensive project needed considerable courage and faith but the Chairman, John Norton, stood firmly with the Headmaster; in 1987 the new House for eighty-five girls went ahead with flexibility at the heart of the planning. Co-education was proceeding apace.

Junior Cross Country.

The Duke of Edinburgh with Hugh Wright in the Library at the time of the opening of Edinburgh House. John Norton, Chairman of Governors, is extreme left, Dick Copas, Second Master, extreme right with, next to him the Bursar, John Russell.

Wright introduced a tutor system and appointed a much-needed Registrar. He created arts priority time for the benefit of music and play rehearsals amongst other activities. The growing number of girls did away with the need for treble voices in the choir and the appointment of Angela Dugdale saw a transformation of choral music within two years. A second choir was soon recruited and The Crickets chamber choir soon earned a reputation locally. Foreign tours were organised and links with choirs from Europe, notably Odessa in the Ukraine, were forged. Before long the main choir was performing in the Royal Festival Hall and winning national competitions. Asked whether he had any regrets about his time at Gresham's, Hugh Wright noted that he would like to have done more teaching and to have got to know the pupils better. Six years was not a long tenure but in that time, assisted by a strong team including the highly efficient and respected Second Master Dick Copas, and with Tony Cuff successfully guiding the thriving Preparatory School, much was achieved and the numbers rose steadily.

In 1991 Hugh Wright moved on to become Chief Master of King Edward's, Birmingham. He was later to become Chairman of HMC. In his place the Governors appointed John Arkell whose experience included National Service as a submariner, a formative East Anglian stint at Framlingham, and Housemastering at Fettes where he was also founding Headmaster of the Preparatory School. He then became Headmaster of Wrekin College in Shropshire. He and Jean, his wife, got off to an excellent start impressing staff and pupils alike by their ability to put names to faces. They had done their homework well.

Following a difficult first year during which he had to part company with several senior pupils and to deal with a group of disaffected Sixth Formers, John Arkell found that numbers in the Senior School had slipped a little. Partly because of this and partly to maintain academic standards and improve Music and Art,

The Cairns Centre.

In the Howson's Common Room.

Pupils behind bars.

Arkell persuaded the Governors to increase markedly the scholarships available. Sports Scholarships followed and also the more contentious continuation scholarships payable at 11 and designed to secure good pupils whilst they still had two years to go in their preparatory schools. Accepting the need to generate sufficient surpluses to fund the major building projects planned, the Governors, despite considerable misgivings, raised fee levels far above the normal incremental level in 1996/7. Few parents complained though many must have felt the pinch. The Headmaster was able to argue that comparable schools, including several in the eastern region, were still more expensive and that the planned programme would give their children facilities second to none. This minor crisis soon passed and numbers rose again to well over 500 in the Senior School assisted by the unfortunate closure of Runton Hill. Runton had amalgamated with Sutherland House, another girls' school, in Cromer, which had closed its doors earlier and now there was no independent alternative for girls in north Norfolk. It was a sad moment because Gresham's had maintained cordial relations with Runton through the regular attendance of individual girls in Science Sixth-Form classes for many years. The years 1991–1993 could have been far worse from the point of view of cash flow had it not been for the steadiness of the Junior School's numbers at the time.

One difficult and unpopular decision which John Arkell had to take was the closure of Old School House as a Senior Boarding House in 1993. Boys' numbers had fallen by around thirty in the preceding three years and it was becoming increasingly difficult, despite the excellent work done by the Housemaster, Norman Semple, and his wife, Jan, to persuade new parents to place their sons in the town with the regular lengthy walk or bicycle ride to the main site. Feelings ran high and current parents sought a meeting with the Chairman, Antony Butterwick, whose diplomacy carried the day. Fittingly the boys of OSH won the House singing competition in their last year. The shape of recruitment was changing as it was in many other schools. A third girls' house would soon be required and a scheme was discussed for the sale of OSH. This would have caused enormous debate and it was perhaps fortunate that the planning officers were unimpressed.

The cost of a new girls' house, for which the site of the future Theatre was ear-marked, would be manageable only if other projects were placed on hold for several years. And so, for the second time, the Governors looked at the 1938 Sanatorium building beyond Edinburgh. Once it had been thought too remote and even insecure, bordering woodland as it did. However one wing was already being used as an annexe for the overflowing Edinburgh. The rest was home for the relatively new Pre-Preparatory School. For a surprisingly reasonable sum the old 'San' was converted to house a full complement of up to eighty girls with accommodation for a resident married Housemistress. The Pre-Prep took over the main rooms of the Old School House. Benjamin Britten's nephew, Alan, was invited to open Britten House in 1996. He remarked that there might be those (and possibly even the great man himself) who would be amused at the concept of a girls' house being named in his honour. Suitably one of the outstanding pupils of the 1990s was a girl, Sarah Raine, who became Head of School in 1993. Sarah went on to Cambridge, a First in History, Blues in hockey and cricket and the Presidency of the Cambridge Union; thence fast-track to the Foreign Office.

Sport remained strong. Graham Worrall produced some excellent rugby sides regularly competing successfully against schools with greater numbers from which to choose. Alan Ponder continued to work wonders at cricket, undeterred as external examinations crept earlier and earlier in the term. In 2000 he could report thirty-seven wins out of fifty-six matches, played by teams at all levels. Shooting

The hope of his side: the Astroturf.

Richard Leman displays his two Olympic hockey medals before opening the Astroturf pitches in 1994.

Hockey practice before the coming of the Astroturf.

After the opening of the Auden Theatre, the Duke 'plants him a tree' flanked by David Olby and John Arkell.

The Auden pillar.

continued to prosper greatly, as did resurgent sailing crews, and athletics returned to its former standing. Hockey, however, was fighting to hold its place as one of the foremost schools in the east, a position won by successive coaches Max Parsons, Dan Frampton, Steve Benson and David Beeby. Peter Badger, their successor, pushed hard for an artificial-grass pitch for several years. This was by now the standard surface for all club, league, county and national teams. At last authorisation was given in 1994, and, once persuaded, the Fishmongers' Company showed typical generosity by providing additional funds so that two surfaces could be laid at the same time. Gresham's resumed its leading position in the hockey hierarchy quickly joined by the girls' teams. The Prep also reaped great benefit. Few schools could claim facilities such as these, which provided much-needed tennis courts in the summer. In 1999 the Old Greshamian Squash V won the Public Schools' Londonderry Cup for the last time as the Squash Rackets Association decided not to continue the event. From its inception in 1934, Gresham's won the trophy no fewer than thirteen times.

Part of the final interview for the Headship in 1991 had taken the form of a presentation by candidates of their vision for the future of Gresham's. John Arkell, himself an experienced producer and director of plays in previous posts, had highlighted the advantages of a purpose-built theatre/auditorium. Apart from the Theatre-in-the-Woods, the other stages had been either in the Houses (and the author remembers the extraordinary improvisation which provided a tiny stage and rickety raked seating for nearly two hundred in the Woodlands dining room, an arrangement which would have given palpitations to any modern fire officer), in the Main Dining Hall or in Big School. None was really suitable; all were inconvenient. The long tradition of Gresham's drama dating back to Howson's first summer term was a strong argument as was the interest within the school now that Theatre Studies had been placed on the curriculum. An appeal raised £500,000, the Fishmongers gave £200,000, a grant from the Foundation for Sport and the Arts brought in £100,000. The balance was to be raised out of income over fifteen years and the Theatre was opened by the Duke of Edinburgh in 1998. So large and expensive a project could only be justified by the potential good it would bring. Fortunately in Paul Hands the School found a Drama Director who had the vision to make the Auden Theatre a centre for all manner of local groups and touring companies, who brought a diverse programme for the education and entertainment not only of the students, staff and parents but of many theatregoers from all over the county.

It was not only drama which filled the Auden Theatre calendar. Ever since Hugh Wright had asked Angela Dugdale to take over the Choir, the popularity of music had greatly increased. John Arkell succeeded in persuading Mrs Dugdale to become Director of Music for two years and the transformation was completed. The appointment of her charismatic successor Mark Jones ensured that the reputation of Gresham's music was maintained and increased. The auditorium of the Theatre was planned to seat an audience of 300 with a large open stage. The acoustic was ideal for both drama and music. It was this double use which had

*View of the River Thames with London Bridge, the old Fishmongers' Hall and the Royal Barge
by William James (18th Century).* Fishmongers' Hall Collection.

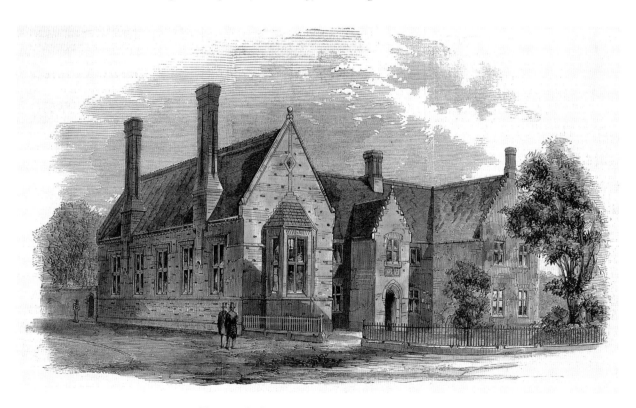

The new school room (1858) of Holt Grammar School.

The Revd David Duncombe's map of the Grammar School (c 1717)
showing damage to the garden wall caused by the great fire of Holt in 1708.

The memorial East window of the Chapel: 'City of Peace' by Reginald Bell.

Above: *Storm clouds over the chapel. Howson's grave is by the south wall.*

Right: *Carol service by candlelight.*

Big School through the 1903 gates.

Girls going back to Britten House.

Oakeley House (incorporating the original 1903 Sanatorium) and garden.

The Auden Theatre by day and by night.

The cricket field.

Big School with the library in the background.

Above: *The Old School House, now the Pre-Preparatory School.*

Far left: *Prep school boarders on the fire-escape at Crossways.*

Left: *Pre-prep at play. The window of the 1858 school-room can be seen in the background.*

Above: *Sixth formers leave Howson's for lessons.*

Right: *Angela Dugdale conducts the strings in the Theatre-in-the-Woods.*

Senior School Staff, 2001.

'Integrated Studies': a medieval banquet in Big School.

John Arkell with pupils on the steps of the Pavilion.

The Auden Theatre from the Headmaster's house.

persuaded the Governors to go ahead with the project in the first place. For any one school to provide five members of the National Youth Choir in a single year, as happened in 1999, speaks volumes for musical standards. And the number of pupils signing up for Theatre Studies at A level and now Dance at the new AS level bear testimony to the bold investment in teachers and theatre staff as well as in the Auden Theatre itself. One example of that success came in 1999 when three pupils (who had all taken Theatre Studies at A level and appeared together in the Gresham's production of *Guys and Dolls* in 1992) received critical acclaim. Sienna Guillory played the lead in a highly acclaimed BBC dramatisation of *Take A Girl Like You*, Sarah Colman (under her stage name Olivia Colman) played Kathleen in *Long Day's Journey into Night* at the Lyric, Shaftesbury Avenue, and Sam Gough was Quasimodo in *Notre Dame de Paris* at the Dominion.

The Britten column ('Hymn to Saint Cecilia').

The 1990s saw the consolidation of certain trends in independent school recruitment and the creation of some more. Co-education proceeded apace as more and more senior and preparatory boys' schools opened their doors to girls. By the year 2000 there was not a single boys' senior school in East Anglia, day or boarding, which did not at least recruit girls into the sixth form. Gresham's' early move in this direction was helpful but other schools were catching up and competition for custom was fierce. A steady increase in the number of girls saw the proportion in the Preparatory School rising from 30 per cent in 1988 to 46 per cent in 1999. In the Senior School the increase in this same period was from 29 per cent to 40 per cent.

Another development was the increasing localisation of intake. This was partly due to the decline in parental demand for boarding but even boarders came increasingly from within a small radius of the school. In 1979 the numbers in the

Conservation work.

Abseiling on Adventure Training.

Preparatory and Senior Schools totalled 557 of whom 61 per cent came from Norfolk. In 1995 that figure had risen to 75 per cent (from a total of 742 pupils) and in 1999 to 78 per cent (from 757). Many relatively affluent families had moved into the county and into north Norfolk in particular over the last third of the twentieth century. At the height of the Howson years, there had been a strongly expressed fear that Gresham's was no longer a Norfolk school. In 1916, of the 230 enrolled pupils, by now predominantly boarders, well over half came from outside Norfolk: from the north of England, from London and from the southern counties. Now, at the end of that same century Gresham's was, once again, largely a 'local' school.

In this climate the role of Gresham's own Junior School became increasingly important. The Junior House has been mentioned from time to time, first under Wynne-Willson in the Old School House, moving to Bengal Lodge (renamed Kenwyn) and then across the road to the new Kenwyn in the 1950s. Numbers had been small throughout the early years of the 20th century though the return from Cornwall saw them rise to 85 (out of 286) in 1945. As the Senior School numbers increased, those in the Junior School remained steady: 80 in 1950, 93 (out of 351) at the end of Martin Olivier's time in 1954. The building of new Kenwyn enabled the numbers to climb from 100 in 1960 to 150 in 1980. The coming of co-education and the further expansion of facilities allied to market forces saw the roll increase to 230 by the end of the century.

Gresham's Youth Theatre at Edinburgh in 2000: 'The End of Innocence'.

The work of John Williams, Michael Hughes and Neville Jones was crucial in laying the foundations for the emergence of Gresham's Preparatory School but it was not until the appointment of Tony Cuff in 1984 that the 'Junior School' took on a separate (though closely linked) identity. The Governors appointed a sub-committee under the Vice-Chairman Henry Jones to oversee this significant development. Apart from its new title, the School was to have its own staff working exclusively with the younger boys (until this time most had had teaching timetables which included classes in both the Senior and Junior Schools) and new buildings were to be erected on the Preparatory School site. Hitherto many classes, especially Science, Art and Technology, had been taught in the Senior School facilities which wasted time and prevented the development of *esprit de corps* and a sense of identity. A new nine-classroom block was opened in May 1985 by the Prime Warden Lord Leverhulme. This gave the Prep plenty of space which was soon needed as numbers rose. The 'Old' Kenwyn classrooms, across the road, were converted to Arts, Technology and Home Economics (Food Technology). There must have been a few wry grins on the faces of the true blue Prep School staff when the Home Economics facilities were enlarged for Senior School pupils as well. The mountain, for once, came to Mohammed.

Extensions to Kenwyn and Crossways in 1985 made it possible to introduce co-education without major fuss by making Crossways the centre for girls, both boarding and day. In 1985 the first two girl boarders arrived, Gemma Keep and Alex Mainstone. In 1991 there were over ninety girls in all and the total numbers were a record 251. By 2000 the proportion of boys to girls was 60:40. The building programme moved apace after 1990 with another classroom block incorporating offices, Library, Hall and Staff Common Room. In 1995 a new Music School

The CCF Band.

Assembly in Big School.

was opened by the Chairman Antony Butterwick, and in 2001 more tennis courts were provided at the same time as the last 'over-the-road' teaching rooms were replaced with a purpose-built Art, Pottery, Design and Information Technology building. Finally a new Science Laboratory was provided to cope with increased demand.

As in the Senior School, the Music and Drama at the Prep gained in reputation as the Millennium approached with Elizabeth Rooke a particular inspiration as Head of the Music Department. Drama now presents three major productions and five year-group performances every year. In 1995 Gresham's Youth Theatre first performed in the Edinburgh Fringe Festival and has done so ever since. On four occasions they have won a Four-Star review in the *Scotsman* and in 2000 they were nominated for a First Fringe Award under the direction of Simon Clarke.

Sport has been strong throughout the last twenty years. The rugby first XV under the coaching of Richard Brearley enjoyed a period of nine years to 1995 during which it was unbeaten in home matches. Graham Britton began an era of great distinction for the Prep hockey teams which four times won the National Mini Hockey Competition and in 1999 no less than twenty-seven boys and girls went through to the National Athletics Finals winning twelve medals including six golds.

In 1984 Tony Cuff was instrumental in persuading the Governors to take over a small pre-prep school run by Penny Moore who was later succeeded by Leslie Gillick. At first it was placed, with twenty pupils, in the old Sanatorium; in 1996 it was moved to the Old School House where, under Daphne Dawson-Smith, it flourishes with a roll of over a hundred.

With full boarding becoming a less popular option for Prep parents, most of whom live within a short distance of Gresham's, weekly boarders and day pupils increased and a successful move was made to hold Chapel on Saturday mornings with many parents opting to attend. The Preparatory School has developed greatly during the last twenty-five years providing a fine all-round education. Twenty

124

years ago only 65 per cent of leavers moved on to the Senior School, but that figure is now close to 100 per cent – crucial to Senior School recruitment and a tribute not only to John Arkell and Tony Cuff and their staff but to the Governors who had the vision to build a fully equipped and hugely successful independent Preparatory School.

John Arkell was granted an extension of three years to his contract as a recognition by the Governors of his outstanding achievement as Headmaster. He retired in 2002. He had guided Gresham's through over a decade of unprecedented educational change due to the reforms of successive governments to leave the school stronger than ever academically and with numbers buoyant. He had also done much for the Arts and to establish a happy, positive and confident ethos. The reputation of the school has never been higher as a new chapter in its history opens with the appointment of Antony Clark, an experienced Headmaster in South Africa who leaves one of his country's leading schools, St Andrew's, Grahamstown, his second Headship, to take up the reins at Gresham's.

Antony Clark.

With the continuing debate about post-GCSE examinations, the inevitability of less favourable financial times in the future, political uncertainties despite the apparent goodwill of the current government, the perennial squalls surrounding the questions of VAT on fees and charitable status, independent schools must be ever watchful. Changes in family life and social fabric have seen the rise of co-education and the decline of boarding, though adaptations of the latter are still popular. The last quarter of the twentieth century illustrates graphically the pace of change in the modern educational world; Gresham's is well placed to meet the challenges of the new century.

Both the founder and the re-founder of Gresham's School would have difficulty in recognising their creation but they would be gratified by its sturdiness and its success. The faithfulness of the Fishmongers' Company, over nearly 450 years, to their promise to Sir John Gresham in 1555, the dedication of successive School Visitors and the determination of several outstanding Headmasters over the centuries, notably Thomas Tallis and John Holmes, kept the flame alive. Finally, George Howson's years of frustration fuelled his vision which the Governors shared and which his heirs, together with generations of staff and pupils, have enlarged over the last hundred years.

Carol service.

One thing remains constant and that is the School's incomparable north Norfolk setting. 'Our lot,' said Howson a century ago, 'has fallen in a fair ground and we are deeply conscious of it.' Few connected with the history of Gresham's School would not say 'amen' to that.

Howard Chatfeild Clarke's original design for the 'new school' buildings (1900).

7

The Early Years 1555–1900

Part I : The School to 1729

The Gresham family settled in north Norfolk before 1360. James Gresham (*c*.1420 –post 1497) lived in Holt, and was the lord of the manor of East Beckham and a cousin of the Pastons. His grandson, Sir John Gresham (*c*.1496–1556), was involved in the textile trade in Antwerp, imported grain from Germany and wine from Bordeaux, and traded with Crete, the Levant and Portugal. He was active in the Worshipful Company of Mercers in London, serving as master on four occasions. He was sheriff of London and Middlesex in 1537-8, and was knighted in the same year. He lent money to, and acted as an agent for, Cardinal Wolsey, through whom he came to know Thomas Cromwell. He had a reputation for ruthlessness.

From 1526, for over twenty years, he was a member of the royal household, firstly as one of the gentleman pensioners to Henry VIII, and later as one of the esquires of the body. These posts were largely honorific and supernumerary. They enabled him to make important connections and to profit from the distribution of monastic properties. In return, the court used him to serve on the juries empanelled to try for treason the associates of Catherine Howard, Henry VIII's fifth wife, and, in 1546, he was one of the commissioners for the survey of the chantries in Surrey, Sussex and Southwark, prior to their suppression and plunder.

Between 1542 and 1548, he helped victual Berwick-upon-Tweed during the Scots' war, provided money, men and materials for Henry VIII's invasion of France, obtained letters of marque to allow one of his ships to prey upon French and Scottish merchant ships as a privateer, and lent the king huge sums of money in return for the mortgages of tracts of crown land. He was also involved in the disastrous policy of debasing the silver coinage with copper, and obtained profitable agencies for the royal monopolies of lead and alum. He served as lord mayor of London between 1547 and 1548. In the reign of Edward VI, he helped to liquidate the royal debt in the Low Countries and as a founder of the Muscovy Company, he provided some of the capital for the voyage of Sir Hugh Willoughby to Russia.

The foundation of the grammar school in Holt was entwined with the history of the Priory of Augustinian canons, founded in 1216, at Beeston Regis near Sheringham. The canons served as parish priests of adjacent livings and kept a school where, as the children of a prominent resident of Holt, Sir John and his

Portrait of Sir John Gresham.

127

brothers were probably educated. In 1535, the Priory's establishment consisted of the prior, four canons, six boys and seven servants. The boys were boarders; their number would have been augmented with day boys. The Priory provided an exhibition for a scholar to study at Oxford. With the suppression of the Priory in June 1539, educational provision for boys in the immediate vicinity of Holt ceased.

As a prominent member of the Mercers' Company, Sir John was involved in the government of four schools: St Paul's and the Mercers' School, London; Collyer's Grammar School, Horsham; and Dauntsey's School, West Lavington, Wiltshire. His two closest business associates and friends were Alderman Sir Rowland Hill (*c*.1492–1561), who founded a grammar school at Market Drayton in Shropshire, and Alderman Sir Andrew Judde (*c*.1494–1558), who founded Tonbridge School in Kent. Sir John's desire to found a school in Holt can be traced to his acquisition of the Priory's manor of Holt Pereers in September 1545. He subsequently purchased his family's ancestral freehold property in Holt from his elder brother in 1546, but business commitments prevented him from making further provision until 1551-2.

It is possible that the educational commitments of the Mercers' Company deter-

Remains of Beeston Priory.

mined Sir John to settle his school's governance into the hands of the Worshipful Company of Fishmongers, with whom he had connections prior to 1551. The school's original statutes were probably drawn up by Thomas Freeman, the high master of St Paul's School between 1549 and 1559, who was well known to Sir John.

By letters patent of 27 April 1555, 1 and 2 Philip and Mary, the school was endowed with the manors of Holt Hales and Holt Pereers, with land in ten other Norfolk parishes, and with three houses formerly in the possession of the Hospital of St Giles, Cripplegate. Work on the new school house began prior to the granting of the first patent. The transfer of the lands to the Fishmongers was confirmed by a deed dated 16 October 1556, seven days before Sir John's death. The endowment of the school fell foul of the Statute of Mortmain, and the case went to the Court of Chancery after Sir Christopher Heydon (c.1519–1579) of Baconsthorpe Castle seized the manor as Sir John's feudal overlord. He was confirmed in its possession and in 1562 he agreed to settle £7 per annum from the profits of the manor on the school in return for the right to nominate its master and usher alternately with the Fishmongers' Company in perpetuity. The school was opened prior to 1 May 1562, and new letters patent were granted by Elizabeth I on 12 July 1565.

The history of the school to 1592 is lost, due to the destruction of the records of the Fishmongers' Company in the Great Fire, and only the surnames of two of the first three masters are known. The Heydon family remained closely involved in the government of the school throughout the remainder of the century. Sir William Heydon (1540–1594) educated his sons there and appointed the fourth master, Christopher Williams (c.1550–1602), prior to 1584. Christopher Williams, although neither a graduate nor a clergyman, belonged to a group of local clergymen who shared books, Puritan views, and met for 'prophesyings' where the Scriptures were expounded. In 1600, Sir Christopher Heydon (c.1560–1623), OG, was obliged to mortgage Baconsthorpe and sold various rights and manors, including the nomination of the master and usher of Holt Grammar School to James Hobart (c.1550–1611) of Norwich.

In 1602, Richard Snoden (1568–c.1619) of Christ's College, Cambridge was appointed the first known graduate master, upon the recommendation of Sir Nathaniel Bacon of Stiffkey and the mayor and aldermen of Norwich. He found the school 'in very weake case'. In return for teaching thirty boys, he was paid £20 per annum for himself and his usher, and lived 'in the great house wherein the schoole is kept'. Snoden had been a schoolmaster in the parish of St Peter Hungate, Norwich in 1597 and tutor to Sir Nathaniel's stepchildren. During his mastership, William Bennett, a fishmonger and the executor of the estate of Leonard Smith, established a closed scholarship from the school to Sidney Sussex College, Cambridge. Snoden was ordained deacon and priest in Norwich in 1604, resigned the mastership in 1605 and later became a prebendary of Carlisle Cathedral.

The Fishmongers considered two candidates for the mastership, Francis Catlyn (c.1580–1624) of Christ's College, Cambridge, who came highly recommended by

The Plaque (above and below) *bearing the arms of the Fishmongers' Company and of Sir John Gresham, above the entrance to the Old School House in Holt. The Plaque dates from the seventeenth century.*

Baconsthorpe Castle.

the Vice-Chancellor, and Thomas Tallis. They appointed the former, but were subsequently informed by Catlyn that Tallis had been appointed by James Hobart. On 17 February 1606, the company decided upon the face-saving expedient that Catlyn should not retain the mastership because he 'is beneficed & hath cure of sowles and cannot with good conscience discharge that & a schoolms place also.' Catlyn had been ordained a deacon by the Bishop of Norwich in 1604 and was made vicar of Briston in 1605. In 1608, he became rector of Thurning, and in 1612, upon his resignation of Briston, was made vicar of Guestwick, which he held, together with Thurning, until his death in November 1624.

Thomas Tallis (*c*.1564–1640), a native of Tugby in Leicestershire, gained his BA at Trinity Hall in 1584, became a notary public, and at one time practised as a proctor (solicitor) in the ecclesiastical courts. He was licensed as a schoolmaster by the Bishop of Norwich in 1597 and taught in Walsingham and Fakenham. When he arrived in Holt, he found the school without a pupil. Tallis secured from the company an allowance of £6 13s 4d (20 nobles) per annum for the salary of an usher, which he may have augmented from the monies received from his private pupils. The school library was improved in 1607 and 1610–1, and during his mastership Tallis sent at least twenty-five boys to Caius College and others to Sidney Sussex, Queens', St John's, and Christ's Colleges, Cambridge.

In November 1617, Tallis notified the company that 'by reason of his age, dymnes of his sight and hearing decayed,' he wished to resign the mastership. The request was denied. On 3 June 1633, James Hobart Junior complained to the company that 'Mr Tallis . . . by reason of his great age and deafnes is not fitt to continue Schoolemr there . . . and that his Usher . . . is neither a scholler nor otherwise fitt to bee Usher.' Mr Hobart suggested two possible replacements, including the Revd Thomas Cooper (1607–1650), the late usher, who in his opinion was 'honest, fitt, and sufficient.' Tallis responded to the charges against him with asperity, particularly the claim that he was 'decrepite, drowsy, sleepie and insufficient to teach,' and commended his usher, Nicholas Davie, who 'taught gramer and other pety latin bookes and most to write . . . and to cipher also . . . he is an ancient man – well stayed, no haunter of alehouses.' He confessed that the school was diminished: 'partly by the multitude of teachers almost in every towne, partly by dearnes of dieting for now none can be boarded under £10 yearly and I never tooke above £7 p. annu[m] neyther of knights, gentlmen nor others.'

The Fishmongers supported Tallis, but the problems which had been highlighted could not be ignored indefinitely. On 7 May 1638, the Fishmongers received a petition from Cooper claiming that the usher's educational deficiencies were such that many of the local gentry were removing their children. The school then had only thirty day boys and no boarders. Cooper asked if he could be admitted usher or assistant to Tallis during his lifetime, stating that 'hee would bee contented that Mr Tallis should sitt still and take his ease . . . and yet Mr Tallis should have and enjoye his stipend of £20 a yeare and his dwellinge in the howse alsoe duringe his life.'

The company ordered Tallis to provide a more learned and able usher for the

SIR JOHN GRESHAM Lord Mayor of London who founded this school A.D 1555

✠ MARY ✠ 1st wife of Sir John Gresham of Holt Norton ✠ She died Sept 21. 1538.

Sir John Gresham and his first wife Mary: windows in the Chapel.

school, and to explain why he had dismissed Cooper. If Tallis is to be believed, Cooper had been far from satisfactory. Between 1629 and 1631, he had acted as curate of Holt before being presented to the rectory of Little Barningham, and Tallis had discharged him as usher at Michaelmas because his negligence and severity 'displeased both the better and meaner sorte,' and because 'of his mean attendance in his place employing him self sometime aboute his p(ar)sonage, sometime upon his pleasures and sometime about other busines not beseming his place.'

Tallis's answers satisfied the company and the matter rested until May 1639 when the Revd Nethanial Gil (1606–1669), a schoolmaster of St Andrew's, Holborn, came to a private arrangement with Tallis. Their relationship was troubled and, when on 31 March 1640 the Fishmongers declined to take sides in their disagreement, Gil resigned the mastership, which reverted to Tallis. In June 1640 Tallis was teaching thirty-five scholars without the help of an usher.

Tallis died on 17 August 1640, bequeathing his volumes of Cicero, Virgil, Horace, Salust, Terence and Ovid, and a Greek lexicon to the school. A monument to him erected in the south aisle of the parish church was destroyed in the fire of Holt in 1708.

131

Tallis's last usher was Henry Luce (*c*.1620–1666), OG, the son of his house-keeper. Luce had acted as usher in 1638 whilst residing in Holt during an outbreak of the plague in Cambridge. He ran the school until a new master was appointed and subsequently gained the patronage of the Paston family, becoming master of their grammar school at North Walsham.

Upon the death of Tallis, Nethanial Gil again petitioned for the mastership but was refused on the grounds that he had a benefice. He was chaplain to the Earl of Dover and to Lady Elizabeth Coke, who had presented him to the living of Burgh-by-Aylsham in 1638. Gil was the son of Alexander Gil senior, high master of St Paul's between 1608 and 1635, who taught Milton. Gil was thrown out of his living for his royalist sympathies in 1644 but continued to preach and take services with the connivance of his parish until the aftermath of the royalist uprising in north Norfolk in 1650, when he settled in Bungay. He was restored in 1660 and in 1663 became rector of Aylsham, retaining the living of Burgh where he died in 1669.

Another unsuccessful petitioner was the former usher, the Revd Thomas Cooper. The governors informed him that they were not willing to have as their school-master any man who had a cure of souls. He took private pupils and remained friendly with the Hobart family, lords of the manor of Holt Market, and was impli-cated with the brothers Edmund and William Hobart (the brothers-in-law of Thomas Witherley, the headmaster between 1640 and 1644) in the abortive royal-ist rising in north Norfolk in 1650. He was captured, condemned to death, and, according to tradition, hanged before the schoolhouse door in Holt on Christmas Day 1650.

The Fishmongers appointed Thomas Witherley (1618–1694) upon the recom-mendation of his maternal uncle, Sir Edmund Reve, and the dean, prebends, mayor and aldermen of Norwich.

In October 1642, it was reported that Holt had been visited with the smallpox and that there had been 'noe schollers . . . since Midsomer last yett the schoole-master hath attended but the usher went away for feare.' In May 1643 the Fishmongers noted that he had neglected the school by 'betaking himselfe to the studie and profession of phisick' and that he wished to leave his post for six months to take a medical degree in Holland. Anticipating their permission, Cooper had himself licensed by the bishop as *ludimagister principalis liberae scola gra-maticals infra p[ar]ochia de Holt* on 14 June 1643. In the end Witherley did not go to Holland and Cooper was not appointed acting master.

The former resigned the mastership in September 1644, and was subsequently appointed by the Royal College of Physicians to serve as a physician during the Great Plague of London. In due course he was knighted, served as Second Physician to Charles II and James II and was President of the Royal College of Physicians from 1684 to 1688. A staunch royalist, he was accused by the Whig his-torian Burnett of trying to subvert the Protestant succession by complicity in James II's plans to introduce a changeling as Prince of Wales. Witherley did not forget the school and sent one of his sons to be educated there in the 1670s.

Witherley recommended as his successor John Fenn (1622–1646) who was probably a native of Gresham, and an old boy of the school. Of 'pious and sober conversation,' he took his BA from Corpus Christi College, Cambridge in 1642–3 and was buried at Holt on 25 June 1646. Once again, Cooper put himself forward for the mastership and was rejected. Richard Breviter (1622–1664) was appointed to the post and sent to be examined in Latin and Greek by John Langley, the high master of St Paul's, and William Dugard, the head master of Merchant Taylors', who found him 'soe farre below their expectacon and in such a condicon as made them wonder hee should offer himselfe to the imploymt of a schoolemrs place in a publiq gramm[ar] schoole.'

Finally, in August 1646, the Revd Francis Wright (1609–1659), was appointed master. He was educated at Eton and Merton College, Oxford, where he was a fellow from 1631 to 1650 and one of the college's lecturers in Greek. A royalist, Wright had written verses commemorating the king's recovery from smallpox in 1633 and remained in Oxford throughout the time that the city was garrisoned for the king. He left the city before the parliamentary commissioners ejected all those whose loyalty to the new regime was suspect.

During his mastership, we have the first record of a school captain (1648), although the company's minutes remain preoccupied with leases, the wood and timber belonging to the manor of Holt Pereers, and the repair of the school's well and windows. In 1657, officers of the Fishmongers' Company travelled from London in two coaches and by horseback to visit the school, and their lands in Holt and Hunworth. The journey took four days. The twenty-five free scholars

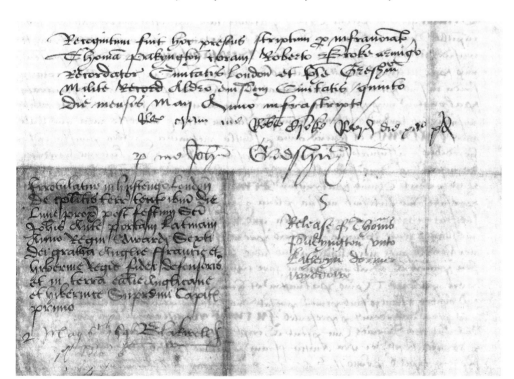

Signature of Sir John Gresham witnessing document dated May 1547.

133

were publicly examined by the Revd John Bond, the Puritan minister of Holt, and Mr Wright was commended for their performance. He was buried in Holt on 6 February 1659.

The company appointed as his successor the Revd William Hickes (1621–1677), formerly of Westminster School and Trinity College, Cambridge. Hickes was a committed Anglican and royalist. He was master of Oundle between 1646 and 1651, when he was 'drove out by ye Presbyterians &c for keeping his schollars to ye prayers of ye church' and his application for the mastership of Stamford School, Lincolnshire (1657) was rejected for similar reasons. His loyalties caused him numerous problems at Holt, and charges were laid against him by Colonel Robert Jermy of Bayfield, who had taken a major role in the suppression of the royalist rising in north Norfolk in 1650. Hickes was unable to obtain a testimonial as to his 'carriage and behaviour' from the Revd John Bond of Holt or 'any other ministers or men of quality.' He resigned on 12 March 1660. Hickes died rector of Downham, Cambridgeshire. He was a maternal uncle of Sir Hans Sloane (1660–1753), the founder of the British Museum.

Henry Mazy (1640–1677) was the son of a Cambridge innkeeper and educated at the Perse School and Caius College. He took his BA in 1658, became usher of Holt Grammar School and was elected master in 1660. He was examined by the head masters of Merchant Taylors' and the Charterhouse, who believed 'if hee be industrious and diligent in his studyes hee may soe improve them that hee may prove a good instrument for the educacon and instruccon of youth.' Not liking their report, the Fishmongers grudgingly confirmed Mazy's appointment 'to satisfy the ministers, gent[lemen] and townesmen in and neere Holt . . . whoe soe earnestly desire him,' although it was subsequently learned that approbation was not universal.

During Mazy's mastership, the library at Holt was augmented by the Fishmongers with books 'bound upp with this Companyes armes, and alsoe chaynes and a deske for those Bookes to be constantly kept att Holt Schoole for the benefitt of the schoolemaster, usher and schollers there.' Very little is known of Mazy's mastership, except that soon after his appointment he made his college friend, John Goodman (1640–1699), usher. Mazy combined the mastership with a junior fellowship at Caius College between 1661 and 1665. He was ordained a deacon at Norwich Cathedral in September 1661, priest in July 1662, and resigned the mastership in 1665 to become master of Norwich Grammar School. Gout in his hands and feet caused a diminution in his activity and the dissatisfaction of his pupils, who termed themselves 'Vulcan's servile bondslaves'. He was presented to the rectory of Rockland near Norwich in 1667, and to the sinecure rectory of Egmere in 1670. He made his will on 14 May 1677 and died three days later, still master of Norwich Grammar School. Mazy was a great-great-uncle of the poet William Cowper (1731–1800).

After Mazy's departure from Holt in June 1665, the school was run by the usher, Goodman, who combined his duties with being curate of Great Ryburgh. What was intended to be a short interregnum lasted two years. The Great Plague result-

Books from the Foundation Library.

ed in the suspension of the meetings of the Fishmongers in the middle of 1665. In September 1666 Fishmongers' Hall and the company's minute book from July 1664 until September 1666 were destroyed in the Great Fire, and the company met in one of the rooms at Bedlam until 14 December 1669.

It was not until 6 June 1667 that the company was able to elect a successor to Mazy. Goodman was paid a gratuity of £8 and subsequently became rector of Themilthorpe (1671) and Twyford (1679), where he was buried on 6 December 1699. The new master, the Revd Thomas Bainbridge (1642–1714), was educated at Kirby Lonsdale Grammar School and Christ's College, Cambridge, and licensed by the Bishop of Norwich to teach grammar, writing and arithmetic at the school.

The earliest surviving statutes for the governance of the school date from the latter part of Bainbridge's mastership (1689) and were drawn up by Dr Thomas Gale (c.1635–1702), the high master of St Paul's and later Dean of York. They were probably closely based on the earlier, and now lost, original, and were subsequently revised by Dr Gale in 1691. From them we learn that the master's salary for teaching classics to the thirty free Sir John Gresham scholars was still the £20 per annum allowed in 1562. This small salary was augmented by the use of six acres of land and the garden and outbuildings behind the school house. The master was also allowed to take as many boarders and paying or pensioner scholars as he liked. They were drawn from a higher social class than the free scholars.

The usher opened the school house door at 6.00 a.m., lessons began after prayers at 7.00 a.m., continuing until 11.00 a.m., and resumed between 1.00 and 5.00 p.m. Before dismissal, prayers were said for Sir John Gresham and the Worshipful Company of Fishmongers, 'every scholar kneeling on his knees devoutly.' The usher then found some boys to sweep the school house and to close the doors at 6.00 p.m. On Saturdays, lessons finished at 3.00 p.m.

Dr Thomas Gale.

The master and usher were to abstain from alehouses and all unlawful games. A scholar could be punished if he came to school with 'head uncombed, his hands and face unwashed, his nose or shoes uncleanly, apparel torn or not well girt unto him.' One or two 'discreet' scholars were appointed monitors and noted all misdemeanours. On Sundays, all the scholars sat together in the school pew in the parish church, under the supervision of the usher and writing master. The usher kept the record of admissions, but none survives prior to 1729. Owing to the difficulty of keeping the school under their personal surveillance, the Fishmongers appointed local visitors to make yearly visits.

In twenty-five years, Bainbridge sent nineteen pupils to Caius, seven to Christ's, and three to St John's. They came from a wide social background and included the sons of local tradesmen, small farmers, and local gentry.

In 1675 Bainbridge accepted the curacies of Matlask and Plumstead, near Holt, which he was allowed to hold in plurality. In 1682, he was also presented to the livings of Salthouse and Kelling. The combined responsibilities of four livings and the mastership proved to be a heavy burden, and people wrote to complain about the poor running of the school. In his defence, Bainbridge claimed that he was doing all that he could to promote the interests of the school but that the local inhabitants were poor and sent their sons to work as soon as possible, and there were many new schools in the area.

The Fishmongers subsequently found Bainbridge guilty of receiving money from the free scholars, contrary to the desire of the founder and the statutes. He attended a court of the Fishmongers on 20 December 1691, was dismissed and was required to leave the school house by Lady Day 1692. Bainbridge died, leaving a much encumbered estate, and was buried at Letheringsett on 7 December 1714.

On 5 April 1692, three candidates for the mastership were examined and William Reynolds (1667–1719) was elected. Born at Aston Rowant, Oxfordshire, the son of the parson, he attended Pembroke College, Oxford, graduating BA in 1690 and MA in 1693. Whilst there, he came to the notice of the master, Dr John Hall (1632–1711), Bishop of Bristol, who recommended Reynolds to the Fishmongers. The partial Jacobite historian, Hearne, claimed that Dr Hall only gave such patronage to low church Whigs: 'twas to none but men of rebellious principles that he bestowed his charity.' We know practically nothing of Reynolds's time at school. Dr Radford (1908), followed by Linnell (1955), claimed incorrectly that it was interrupted by the mastership of Edward Reynolds, from 1697 until 1702. In April 1692, the Fishmongers confirmed the salary of £10 per annum to be paid to a writing master, and in 1699–1700 it was noted that the master's salary was now £30 per annum, '£10 more than any master before him.'

Reynolds described the destruction of the town of Holt by fire on Saturday 1 May 1708 in a letter to the Fishmongers. It has not survived but some details are preserved in a royal brief circulated in 1723 to obtain money for those ruined by the fire. 'A sudden and lamentable fire . . . in the space of three hours, burnt down to the ground almost the whole town and the parish church.' From a plan of the schoolhouse made by Reynolds's successor, we know that the fire lapped the wall enclosing the garden of the schoolhouse, causing several breaches, burning the school's stables, the master's barn and outhouses but mercifully sparing the schoolhouse itself.

Between 1692 and 1716, Reynolds sent twenty-five boys to Caius College and one to Christ's College, Cambridge, besides others who are not recorded. Of those sent to Caius, six became fellows of the college, an academic achievement not equalled or surpassed until Howson's mastership (1900–1919). Reynolds was appointed rector of Sharrington by Holt in 1694 and in 1715 received the additional rectories of Plumstead and Matlask. He resigned the mastership in 1716 and died on 28 October 1719 aged 52, and was buried at Holt.

On 7 March 1716, three candidates were examined for the vacant mastership and the Fishmongers appointed the Revd David Duncombe. Born and educated in Arbroath, he studied philosophy and divinity at the University of St Andrews, obtaining an MA. According to him, he was 'a licenciate for the ministry; but denying to subscribe the [Westminster] confession of the kirk . . . I came to London and setled in teaching the Latin and the Mathematics and by . . . my care and industry . . . my business brings me in £100 per annum.' Between 1707 and 1711, Duncombe kept a school in the parish of Little Minories, and from 1711 to 1715 at St Mary's, Whitechapel. He was ordained a deacon at St Paul's Cathedral on 24 September 1715 but his hopes of returning to Scotland were frustrated by the Jacobite rising in favour of James III.

Part of his time at the school was taken up with repairing the damage caused by the fire of Holt. In c.1717–20 he drew three maps of the schoolhouse which show the damage caused to the wall, orchard and outhouses. In 1715 the church was re-seated and a document dated 5 May 1727 records the allocation of the newly made pews. The 'scole house pew' was the first in the north aisle and in the gallery there was 'the end seate to ye east for ye scole boyes' where they kept company with the charity children and apprentices.

Duncombe resigned the mastership with effect from Lady Day 1729. The date and place of his death are unknown. He was the last clerical master and, with the exception of John Knox (1760), the last graduate to govern the school until Pullan in 1809.

Part 2: 1729–1809

There are more documents extant on the life of John Holmes, the master from 1729 to 1760, than on any other master of the eighteenth century, although we lack details of his early life. By his own account, he was born on Christmas Day 1702. His birthplace is unknown but he was not a native of Norfolk, nor is he known to have been a graduate. In c.1726 he became usher at Holt school, but did not stay long and became a master of the small school run by the Company of Coopers at Ratcliff in Middlesex. He was elected master on 5 February 1729. He was described as 'one who will not . . . encumber himself with any cures or ecclesiastical promotion [which] hath been found, by experience, to be greatly prejudicial and . . .

Board commemorating the visitation of 1729 when John Holmes became Headmaster.

brought the said school into disrepute.'

On 4 June 1729 the prime warden, six of the court of assistants, the clerk and company carpenter left London to visit the school. On the journey, an 'unhappy accident . . . befell the said visitors . . . in being took by three highwaymen in Epping Forest who took from them their money, watches, horses and several other things of considerable value.' Two of the highwaymen were caught and 'committed to the next assize at Chelmsford for robbery.' The most lasting result of the 1729 visitation was that the company 'at their costs and charges provided and furnished the said shool with a valuable and usefull library of the best Latin and Greek authors' and a pair of globes. In February 1731, local visitors reported that the school was flourishing and commended Holmes's diligence.

Holmes made good use of the library and settled down to work writing Latin and Greek grammars. On presenting the company with his new Latin grammar, he was rewarded by a gratuity of ten guineas 'as an encouragement to his diligence and industry in his promoting the credit and reputation of the said school and also the welfare and advantage of the scholars under his charge and care.' The grammar was highly influential in its day and reached an eleventh edition in 1771. In 1734 he published his Greek grammar, which enjoyed great popularity and a revised sixth edition was printed in 1757. *The Lives of the Professors of Gresham College* (1740) by John Ward, FRS, Professor of Rhetoric at Gresham College, notes: 'Mr John Holmes . . . has recommended himself to the Public by his Latin and Greek Grammars.' In 1755, Holmes stated that he had 'within a few years sold about 6,000 Latin Grammars and near 4,000 Greek Grammars.' This was a large circulation for the period and, at 1s 6d for each Latin grammar and 2s 6d for the Greek, Holmes prospered.

The earliest surviving advertisement for the school comes from the 1735 edition of the Greek grammar: 'At Holt in Norfolk, in a large commodious house, pleasantly situated, young gentlemen are boarded and completely qualified for all manner of business in Latin, Greek, Arithmetick in all its parts, book keeping in double entry and called merchants accounts and writing in all the hands used in Great Britain, by the author and proper assistant.' About this time Holmes became associated with one of the most famous historical works of his time, *The History of Norfolk* by the Revd Francis Blomefield (1705–1752). The rector of Holt, the Revd Dr Henry Briggs (1683–1748), Holmes and Dr Edmund Newdigate MD (1702–1779), OG, supplied Blomefield with local information.

The 1730s were halcyon days for the school. It enjoyed an excellent local reputation and drew pupils from all sections of society. There were often over seventy pupils, with thirty free scholars and the remainder pensioner day boys or boarders who paid for their instruction. In that decade ten boys took up Norfolk scholarships at Caius, two went to Pembroke and one each to Corpus, Clare, Jesus and Peterhouse Colleges in Cambridge, and one to Oxford University.

In 1736 Holmes published *The History of England*, based on a performance by the boys at the school's breaking up at Christmas in 1735, and dedicated to Colonel Augustus Earle of Heydon Hall, whose 9-year-old son, Erasmus, entered the school

Erasmus Earle, FSA, Fellow of Peterhouse, Cambridge, Head boy of the School and a favourite pupil of John Holmes.

in 1736 and quickly became Holmes' favourite pupil. Holmes composed a number of pieces of this kind for the public 'Breaking Ups' each Christmas. In 1738 Holmes published the first part of a highly influential work on public speaking, the *Art of Rhetoric*, the second part of which finally appeared in 1755. Its publication coincided with that of his *Clavis Grammaticalis: a key to . . . the Latin and Greek Grammars (1739)*.

In 1741, Holmes informed the Fishmongers that he intended to teach French in the school using his new French grammar, again inscribed to Colonel Earle. 'The French tongue,' he wrote, 'being at this day almost Universal, and consequently in such high repute everywhere for its usefulness in Professions . . . to the end that nothing might be wanting to complete your son and the young gentlemen under many care, I have with the strictest application compos'd these rudiments from close observation of the Genius of that language . . .' In 1936, D.H. Greatwood, a master at Gresham's, noted that Holmes 'takes particular care to teach the pronunciation of the language, but his methods are inevitably very rough and ready.' The grammar ends with a number of readings in French and English, including a dialogue between two speakers called John and Erasmus.

In 1751 he published *The Grammarian's Geography and Astronomy*, finely illustrated with copperplate engravings. Holmes claimed that it was 'particularly adapted to the capacities of young gentlemen studying the classics.' It is dedicated to his 'dearly loved pupils at Holt' whom he lists with their various occupations, going some way to replacing the missing admissions records for the school from 1742 to 1760. He adapts Locke's concept of 'Connection of Ideas' and uses a pack of cards to 'help the memory in recollecting describing and remembering all the places of the terraqueous globe.' Hearts were used to describe Europe, diamonds Asia, spades Africa, and clubs America. The following extract shows Holmes' humour and critical attention to the information he had received:

> The knave of clubs, appearing somewhat like the picture of a cannibal, puts me in mind of the suppos'd Country of the Cannibals – Magellanica or Patagonia, the remotest part of the continent of America, a very barren and much unknown land of a triangular form . . . as to Cannibals . . . we have found none for this 100 years past. That people may have eaten one another . . . driven to it by famine may possibly be true but 'tis hard an instance or two of this nature, should be thought sufficient to denominate a whole country cannibals.

The work also deals with astronomy and the use of the celestial globe. Holmes believed that the planets were inhabited, and in this work he explains, with undeniable logic, his reasons for this belief.

During the period 1745–1755 Holmes also wrote *The Grammarian's Arithmetic; or, A Compendious Treatise of the Art of Cyphering in all its branches both vulgar and decimal*. It was to be printed in four parts and the first appeared in 1751. It is not known if the others were written, and none appear to have survived. In 1755 the Fishmongers presented Holmes with thirty guineas for his *A Second Impression/Corrected and Improved of The Art of Rhetoric*, first printed in 1738. As with his other works, this was intended for grammar schools 'especially in this

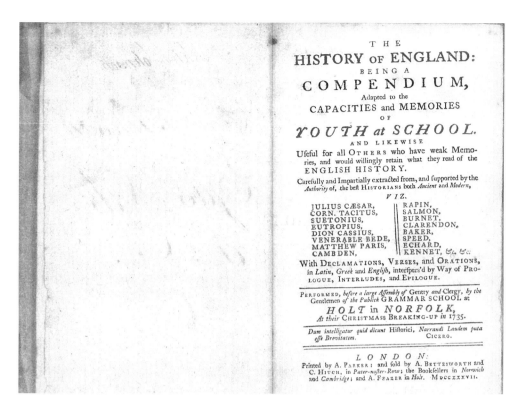

Title page of The History of England *by John Holmes.*

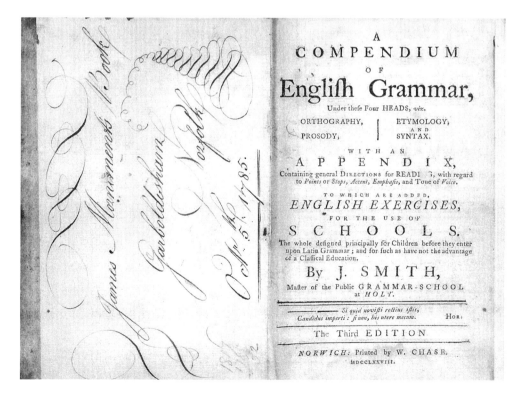

Title page of An English Grammar, for Those Without Latin, *by James Smith.*

Day, when school boys are to be led, sooth'd and entic'd to their studies by the easiness and pleasure of the practice rather than by force or harsh discipline drove as in the Days of Yore.' This was his most influential work and was in print in England and America until the 1840s.

During the 1740s and 1750s the school underwent a gentle decline. In 1759 the Fishmongers visited the school for the first time in thirty years. The original report on the visit has not survived but an extract is preserved in a document of 1813. The visitors were: 'concerned to find so few scholars at the school, there being but about a 1/3rd part of the numbers there ought to be of free scholars (10) and no other scholars whatsoever, that there has not been any usher or writing master for several years past, that there are not any statutes or ordinances in the school for the management or government thereof and it seems to us that for want thereof the annual visitors are in a great measure ignorant of the nature of the duty of their visitation, that the school is in a declining state which we were informed of by several persons at Holt has been the case for several years from the neglect and bad conduct of the master who appeared to us to be greatly impaired and very insufficient for the government of the school; the low reputation of which we think must be speedily retrieved to present the total ruin of it.'

William Hippesley, the clerk to the Fishmongers and a friend of Holmes for many years, was so concerned at the report that he wrote to the Revd Zurishaddai Girdlestone (1720–1767), OG, rector of Bodham and Baconsthorpe, requesting him to persuade Holmes to resign because 'I shall be sorry to have him dismist,' not least of all because this disgrace would affect the marriage prospects of Holmes's only child, Jane. On 8 February 1760, the Fishmongers considered 'the remonstrance and petition of Mr John Holmes offering to resign his place (from Michaelmas) and praying to be allowed one hundred guineas towards building him a house and to be chosen a visitor of the School.' His resignation was accepted but his other requests were rejected. Holmes died on 22 December 1760 aged 57, leaving a widow who survived him by six-and-a-half years. The monument to her memory states that 'the children ever experienced a maternal tenderness, and the parents a conscientious attention to their persons and morals.'

Monument in Holt Parish Church to John Holmes and his wife Jane.

From the nine candidates for the vacancy, John Knox, MA, master of the Corporation Grammar School at King's Lynn from 1755 to 1760, eager to escape the notoriety of having appointed a murderer (Eugene Aram) as his usher, was appointed to succeed Holmes but it is unlikely that he ever resided in Holt. It was reported to the Fishmongers on 10 October 1760 that he had declined the post, accepting more lucrative employment elsewhere. The Fishmongers advertised the post again but it was not until 5 December 1760 that three candidates were examined and James Smith (1725–1794), the non-graduate master of a school in Mattishall, Norfolk, was appointed master.

In 1761 the School's 1689–1691 statutes were revised by the masters of St Paul's and Merchant Taylors'. The local visitors were strengthened by the addition of local clergymen and gentry, almost all of whom were OGs. Relations between the master and the clerk of the Fishmongers were cordial and Smith sent him gifts of braces of pheasants from time to time. Detailed attendance figures have survived for the school between December 1765 and December 1786 and these range between fifty and eighty-eight boys. However, the school only had its full quota of thirty free scholars in 1765, 1766 and 1776, and the number dropped to fourteen in 1783. The Fishmongers visited the school in June 1773, four travelling on horseback and the remainder in three coaches. All was found to be in good order. The visitation in August 1783 was equally successful. On this occasion, the boys performed part of a masque on the subject of 'Moral Tendency' and the governors gave 5s to the head boy and 2s 6d each to the remaining boys, and two days' holiday.

Mrs Ann Smith, wife of James Smith (Headmaster 1760–1787), School Matron.

Smith wrote Latin and English grammars which were widely used in his lifetime. Norwich Library, until its recent fire, held the most complete collection of them to be found anywhere. The School has a third edition of his *Compendium of English Grammar* (1778), devised for children before they began Latin grammar, and 'for such as have not the advantage of a classical education.' Although the school was full, the educational standard seems to have been less demanding and of the boys admitted to the school between 1761 and 1781, only four went on to Caius, two each to Christ's, Sidney and Pembroke, and one each to Corpus and St John's, Cambridge. The teaching of Latin and Greek, although specified in the Statutes, was not universal. Smith resigned the mastership from Michaelmas 1787. The *Norwich Mercury* for 24 January 1794 records his sudden death on 'Tuesday last . . . while taking his afternoon tea, occasioned by a palpitation of the heart, an disorder with which he had been some years afflicted . . . He was exemplary in the discharge of all the relative duties of life and respected as a worthy member of society and a good classical scholar.'

His successor, Thomas Atkins (1756–1814), a non-graduate, was master of a school in Yarmouth on the Isle of Wight. He was examined and found suitable by the high master of St Paul's and the head master of Merchant Taylors'. The records of his mastership are deficient and no register of admissions has survived for the period 1783–1809. In 1799 the Fishmongers visited the school and found it in a poor condition. There were eleven boarders, twenty pensioner scholars and a mere five free scholars. It transpired that the school's rules and orders had not been read, or observed, for many years and, after examination, none of the boys 'appeared to be sufficiently advanced in learning.' The mode of teaching laid down in the Statutes had not been observed and, when challenged, Atkins stated that he understood that free scholarships were 'only extended to the boys of parents of the poorest sort.' An admonition brought temporary relief. The schoolmaster's salary was increased from £40 to £50 from midsummer 1800 and he was allowed to teach any Latin or Greek text that he wanted. No boy was to be admitted to the school who could not read a chapter of the Testament. In 1802, a 'progressive improvement' in the school and in the number of scholars was reported.

In June 1806 Atkins was dismissed for incurring unauthorised expenditure and for misrepresenting the number of scholars in order to profit by the *per capita* bounties by £55 or £60 per annum. Atkins appealed against their decision and won the support of Sir Jacob Astley (1756–1817) of Melton Constable, the Rt. Hon. William Windham (1750–1810) of Felbrigg (a local visitor since 1781 and one-time Secretary of State for War), the Revd Joshua Smith (1758–1828), Rector of Holt, OG, and numerous others. The appeal process dragged on from October 1806 until January 1807. Atkins was found to have behaved in 'a most improper and reprehensible manner' and was reproved in person by the prime warden. He was reappointed master on trial for a year, and required to teach Latin, which had lapsed. Atkins was finally dismissed with effect from Christmas 1809 for not observing the rules and orders of the school and being found 'unworthy' of the continued patronage of the Fishmongers. Atkins printed an address to his friends and the public outlining his efforts on behalf of the school, stating that his dismissal did not reflect upon 'his competency or moral character,' and that the full number of thirty scholars had then been maintained for some years. He gave notice of his intention to conduct a private seminary, and subsequently became master of the grammar school at Aylsham. He died on 23 September 1814 and, with the permission of his friend, the Rector of Holt, a Latin inscription to his memory and talents was placed in the nave of Holt church, adjacent to the schoolhouse pew. From here the scholars and usher could contemplate the life of a 'hard-working master [who was a] watchful son of the Church of England, truly learned, conscientious, upright, unassuming, retiring, deliberately friendly and truly lamented.'

The Governors subsequently found that many of the problems experienced by Atkins in observing the requirements of the 1761 Statutes were valid and that further revision of the Statutes was essential. In the meantime, the removal of Atkins caused much local resentment, the resignation of six of the nine local visitors (leaving only two active visitors) and the departure of most of the boarders and pensioner scholars, who continued their education with Mr Atkins in Aylsham.

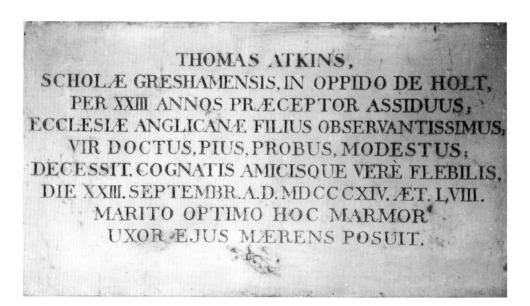

Monument in Holt Parish Church to Thomas Atkins (Headmaster 1787–1809).

Part 3: 1809–1900

In this difficult situation, the Governors advertised for a replacement more widely than at any time since the practice commenced in 1760. They appointed the Revd Benjamin Pullan (1785–1861). He was born at Scarborough, the son of a merchant, and educated at Queen Elizabeth I Grammar School, Wakefield and Clare College, Cambridge, graduating BA (1808) and MA (1811), and holding the Scarborough fellowship between 1808 and 1809. The Fishmongers were aware of the problems that their new master faced in the local community. They visited the school in January 1810 and dined the boys and their supporters at The Feathers, explaining their reasons for removing Atkins.

Pullan found thirty free scholars and three pensioner scholars at the school but by 1813 only ten free scholars, who were taught English and writing, remained. It was found that Latin and Greek were useless for their future occupations. A committee was set up to find remedies to stem the school's decline. The shortfall in the number of visitors was made good in 1811 when a further eight, including a number of OGs, were appointed. Dr Henry Bathurst (1744–1837), the Bishop of Norwich, was consulted, and expressed his 'entire approbation of all that had been done.' In 1815 the number of free scholarships was increased to fifty and new statutes were implemented in 1822. By 1825 the visitors reported 'a palpable improvement in the whole concerns of the school.' Few boys went to university however, and in 1824 it was noted that the Smith Scholarship at Sidney Sussex College had been 'vacant beyond remembrance.'

Pullan's salary was based on the number of fifty free scholars (£100 per annum) to which was added gratuities for the first, second, third, fourth and fifth Latin classes (£21), with an allowance of 15s per annum per scholar for writing books, pens, ink, and paper (£37 10s) and an allowance for coal. To augment his salary, Pullan accepted the curacies of Blakeney and Cockthorpe (1811). He subsequently became vicar of Upper Sheringham (1825) which he served with the curacy of North Barningham until relinquishing the latter to become perpetual curate of Weybourne in 1845. The usher's salary was a mere £50 per annum plus £30 for board and lodging. The Revds Thomas Beckwith and William Robert Taylor were successive ushers between 1821 and 1843. Both were graduates and divided their time between the school and parish duties. The latter combined his post with the perpetual curacy of West Beckham, the chaplaincy of its workhouse and the rectory of Town Barningham. Subsequent ushers had more meagre academic attainments. William Allen Rudkin combined his school duties with being the town's grocer, fruiterer, confectioner, draper and tea dealer.

Pullan was an antiquarian, and he changed his surname to its more historical form, Pulleyne, in 1823. He took a scholarly interest in Roman Norfolk, ecclesiastical remains, and the Palgraves of Barningham. Politically he was 'one of the greatest Tories in these parts,' supporting the Duke of Wellington's Government at a time of great unpopularity. Of commanding appearance, with blonde hair and

The Revd Benjamin Pullan (later Pulleyne) Headmaster 1809–1857. Portrait (1834) by Henry Howard, RA when Pulleyne was 49.

145

The Grammar School before rebuilding c.1850.

pale blue eyes, Pullan was a ladies' man. Larry Banville, gamekeeper to Lord Buxton, described Pullan's roving eye whilst preaching and in 1833 noted that whenever Pullan went to preach at Barningham, he 'stops for tea at Mr Partridge's, a farmer's, and takes away one of his daughters, keeps her out until 11 o'clock, sometimes later. What a shame!' What poor, blind Mrs Pullan thought of this is not recorded. Twenty years later, with indecent haste four months after his first wife's death, the couple were married at New Buckenham, away from spiteful gossip.

Pullan was a strict disciplinarian. The Visitors' Minute Book records a number of expulsions from causes as diverse as non-attendance, contumacy, and non-attendance at church. Edmund Dawson Rogers (1823–1910), a founder of the Society for Psychical Research, was educated on the classical side of the school between 1831 and 1840. He says of his education:

> Nearly all my education and training was in Latin and Greek, to the almost complete omission and neglect of every other subject. We had . . . only two afternoons for other subjects . . . The Eton Latin Grammar was placed in my hands on the first day that I attended school. This Latin Grammar was itself in Latin, so that in reality one ought to have understood Latin before one began to learn it. The general order of things was for the classes to go up to the Headmaster's desk, standing around him on a little raised platform, where we had to repeat these rules in Latin . . . For my failure to please the master in repeating these lessons I suffered considerably, and as the master had a strong penchant for the use of the cane and birch, I was frequently punished so severely that I could not sit down in my seat. Many a time I have seen boys held down over the desk by two other boys and thrashed with a birch rod.

The non-classical side of the school had a wider range of instruction. In 1823, Pullan requested permission to teach geography, navigation, mathematics, geometry, mensuration and land surveying. Shorthand may also have been taught. During his mastership there were few boarders (five in 1824), and from 1830 those who needed accommodation resided in the homes of those on the master's list of approved lodgings. In the 1820s and 1830s the school still educated children of the local gentry, the most important of whom were the two sons of Captain Frederick Marryat (1792–1848) of Langham, whose novels greatly influenced Joseph Conrad and were 'one of the causes of his desire to become an English sailor.'

Pullan's mastership of the school was legendary. Thomas Heywood (1861–1941), in his unpublished autobiography entitled *Tommy, his Tale*, written in the 1870s, recounted the school experiences of his father Horace Heywood (1832–1897), a brewer and wine merchant, who was there between 1843 and 1846: 'In Pa's time the headmaster of Gresham . . . larruped the lads with right good will . . . With . . . added dignities his name mysteriously changed to Pulleyne . . . He seems to have disliked Mr Pullan exceedingly, and Mr Pulleyne still more. He called him a wicked old pluralist . . . [and a] sanctified sadist.'

Not all former pupils were hostile to Pullan. The head boy between 1857 and 1858, William Ransome Mesney (1839–1914), later archdeacon of Sarawak, who translated much of the *New Testament*, the *Psalms* and the *Book of Common Prayer* into Sea Dyak during a demanding thirty years of missionary work, punctuated by bouts of dysentery and beriberi, attributed his linguistic skills to the training he received in Latin and Greek. The Visitors' Book notes a small number of boys during Pullan's mastership who had outstanding linguistic abilities. Few, however, progressed directly to the universities, although occasionally one was awarded an exhibition by the Fishmongers and the Governors found places for boys of promise in commercial establishments. *The Charity Commissioners' Report* (1833) states that 'the school appears to be in great repute.' From 1838 there was a general decline in the standard of classical learning at the school and the visitors condemned the replacement of quill pens with steel nibs. In 1840 the visitors reported, 'we certainly think that such an establishment ought to be productive of more good than it is.'

In 1852 the visitors complained of the 'lack of playground attached to the school from lack of which the boys can only play about the streets of the town, frequently mixing with boys of the lowest class . . . persons of respectability . . . on that account decline sending their sons to the school.' Two years later, the Revd William Upjohn (1774–1855), vicar of Field Dalling, stated 'the school is and has been for years giving proof of a vaste falling off . . . that being a visitor of the National School at Holt, he protests that the boys in that school have a better education than those in the Grammar School.' James Gay (1783–1875), OG, squire of Thurning, attributed the decline to 'the great age of the Revd Benjamin Pulleyne, he being now 69, and his manner of teaching so different from the present period.' The visitors considered the school was intended 'to be for the class at present termed "the middle class of society" and that it should be a school for the sons of gentlemen . . . which at present it is not.'

The endowments of the school yielded almost £350 per annum and the results of the Enclosure Act and the redistribution of the school's properties in Holt between 1807 and 1809 gave it valuable farm land on the Cromer Road which later enabled the school to move out of the town.

Mr Pullan's antagonistic relationship with the Revd Humphrey Jackson, the rector of Holt, came to a head in 1846 when Pullan championed a local hawker, denied a licence by Jackson. He told Jackson, 'You are a disgrace to your profession for depriving an honest family of bread.' There was later a scene at the Fishmongers' dinner at The Feathers. Jackson left in a passion and subsequently tried to have Pullan either disciplined or removed from the school for alleged irregularities. Jackson later drowned himself in the rectory garden in 1853. The surviving diaries of William Repton, attorney of Aylsham, the company's steward of the manor of Holt Perrers, show that the local visitors took their responsibilities of appointing the new scholars and the annual visitation seriously. In 1856 he noted that the visitors heard a complaint against the master, who had severely chastised a boy for reading 'light works from a circulating library.'

In 1857, a deputation from the Fishmongers reported that 'the class of boys had been materially lessening in point of rank of life, and . . . were only fit to be educated in the National School.' Respectable parents would only send their sons to the school if there was a new school building and new staff, and in July the governors were asked to rebuild the schoolroom and build a house for the master which would house twenty boarders. The estimate for this work was considerable, and the company were obliged to take out a mortgage on the trust estates repayable over thirty years. The work was undertaken in two parts: the schoolhouse was reopened on 3 November 1858 and the master's house completed in 1860. At the opening ceremony, attended by the Fishmongers and the local gentry at The Feathers, Mr Pullan summarised the education at the school under his aegis as being 'a happy mixture between the profane and the religious.'

Mr Pullan resigned the mastership at Christmas 1857 'in consequence of his advanced age' and received a small annuity. He retired to the parsonage of Upper Sheringham, where he was remembered as a 'benevolent old gentleman of great charm.' He died suddenly of cerebral apoplexy after taking evening service on 20 October 1861 and was buried in the ruined choir of his beloved monastic church at Weybourne. He was heavily in debt and his possessions were auctioned to meet the demands of his creditors.

The new Headmaster, the Revd Charles Allen Elton BD (1820–1887), son of the recorder of Tiverton, was educated at Blundell's School and Sidney Sussex College, Cambridge, where he was a lecturer and Blundell's Fellow. A fine mathematician, he was tall, blonde, blue-eyed and athletic. His appearance created an instant sensation and he was regarded as 'the catch of the county.' He married Sarah Amelia Ransom (1833–1921), of whom W.B. Yeats' father said, 'she was the handsomest and most impressive woman I ever met.' Elton was described by his

The Revd Charles Elton, Headmaster 1858–67.

GRESHAM

GRAMMAR SCHOOL,

HOLT.

THE REV. C. ELTON, B.D.,

(Late Fellow and Lecturer of Sidney Sussex College, Cambridge,)

Receives BOARDERS into his House.

Terms:—FORTY GUINEAS A YEAR.

THE scheme of instruction includes Classics, Mathematics, and the usual English subjects. German, French, and Drawing are taught by foreign masters on moderate terms.

Each boy has a separate bed. The school house is spacious, and the dormitories are lofty and cheerful. A cricket field, tennis court, and playground are attached to the School.

There are

50 FOUNDATION BOYS,

Who receive their education free of charge, and in addition have their stationery gratis, and books at one third of the publishing price.

These appointments are confined to boys whose parents reside in Norfolk, and preferentially given to those to whom a classical and mathematical education is indispensable.

The Friends of Candidates for nominations must apply to the Head Master for the necessary papers which must be filled up by the parent or guardian of the boy seeking admission. The age must not be less than 8 years.

7

Advertisement for Gresham Grammar School c.1862.

son as 'a Devonshire country gentleman . . . with a taste for open air life, and especially for fishing and for geology: cultivated . . . and with the usual classical tastes and admirations . . . [with] a zest and literary sense which made him fond of translating into verse or prose, from Aristophanes or anyone else.' Canon Walter Marcon (1850–1937), OG, tells us that Mr Elton 'was an exceedingly severe man – literally teaching his class with the cane . . . I've seen a class of say 13 boys at the Headmaster's desk, writhing one after the other until all the whole form were crying.' His recollections are confirmed by Thomas Heywood in almost identical words.

Under his aegis, a cricket field was laid out and fives and tennis courts were built. The old system of public examinations was done away with and replaced by half-yearly written papers, set and marked by the Revds Edward Brumell BD (1815–1901), rector of Holt, and John Fenwick BD (1815–1889), rector of Thurning, who had been fellows of their respective colleges, the former examining in mathematics, the later in classics. The newly established Jodrell prize for mathematics, named after a former rector of Saxingham, helped to encourage and focus attention on this branch of education and the school achieved some notable results in this field in the next forty years. The new usher, Rodney Phillips, was highly regarded and helped the boys to make rapid progress, so much so that he was given notice in order to be replaced by a man with a university degree whose skills would stretch and improve them further. In the resultant fit of depression, Phillips took brandy on an empty stomach before breakfast, passed out, and was immediately discharged. Some of his successors gave little satisfaction. In 1862, Charles Furbank 'abruptly quitted the town leaving considerable debts unpaid,' and his successor, Frederick Dowson, had notice served on him by a solicitor's clerk because 'he does not suit the post and his credentials have quite broken down.' Elton employed a further six second masters between 1863 and 1867, most of whom left due to the inadequate remuneration, or their desire to take holy orders.

French and drawing were introduced into the school in 1859–60 and were taught by a master who was paid by the Headmaster. The French master was not officially on the staff until 1896. In 1860 it was agreed that there should henceforth be two half-holidays, on Wednesdays and Saturdays to foster the school's prowess in sport. Although there was no army cadet force attached to the school prior to Howson, by October 1860 it was reported that forty boys were practising drill under the Rifle Corps' sergeant, and throughout the latter part of the century the Fishmongers were generous patrons of 'I' company of the 3rd Norfolk Rifle Volunteers.

March 1865 was 'so inclement' that better weather, and the desire to escape the stress of the school room, induced Mr Elton to go fishing in the icy waters of the Glaven at Letheringsett. Upon his return, he was confined to bed with rheumatic fever which resulted in partial paralysis in his arms and legs. In the immediate crisis, Mr Brumell assumed the duties of master and acquired the services of William Hooper, who subsequently served as acting master from 1866 to 1867. The

Fishmongers generously helped Elton with his medical fees and the cost of supplying a substitute. In June 1867 they were told by Elton's physician that 'he will be . . . a cripple for life' and, although he was now able to sit up for two hours, he was 'seriously affected by changes in weather.' Mr Elton resigned the mastership from midsummer 1867 and was given a gratuity of £100, and an annuity of £200. The ordeal of his paralysis did not affect his intellect and 'he bore his troubles with remarkable cheerfulness.' He contributed the acrostics to the *Illustrated London News,* which paid him one-and-a-half guineas a week, and he took daily exercise in a hansom cab. He died at Erith, Kent on 17 December 1887, aged 67.

The new master was the Revd Reginald Jolliffe Roberts MA (1833–1911), the son of a minor canon of Chichester Cathedral, who was educated privately in Birkenhead, Wirral and at Christ's College, Cambridge. He was curate of St Mark's, Regent's Park, and mathematics master of the North London Collegiate School, a good water colourist and a conservative. We have a pen portrait of him drawn by Canon Frederic Jarvis, OG. He tells us that 'Bobbie' was 'tall, portly and whiskered. He presided over the big school room . . . and facing him the seniors sat in fours at iron desks doing their work on slates which from time to time they would clean at the bowls of water which stood on the two "tortoise" stoves by which the room was heated. He wielded the cane rarely and temperately . . . There was always much noise in the big schoolroom because such classes as were not working on slates at desks sat on backless benches round three sides of the masters' desks receiving instruction.'

The Revd Reginald Roberts (Headmaster 1867–1900) with the cricket team including John Howell, Second Master (in striped blazer) and William Thorp (holding the ball) Third Master c.1897.

151

Elton had recruited a suitable non-graduate usher at a salary of £80 per annum but this was deemed too small a sum for a graduate, and in 1860 it was raised to £110. This was further raised to £150 in 1873, £180 in 1883, and £200 in 1895. Roberts also had difficulty in retaining his ushers. His first, Robert Stokes (1845–1915), left in 1869 to take holy orders, his second, Robert Campbell Conolly's (1844–1915) 'general conduct necessitated . . . dismissing him' at Easter 1871, and his third, John Lowndes, also left to be ordained. Canon Jarvis described his fifth usher, John Henry Howell, who was in post from 1881 to 1900, as 'blue-eyed, beetle-browed, waxed-moustached . . . whose desk stood half-way down the room . . . from which he would emerge with silent swiftness and wildly thrash the neck and shoulders of some unfortunate boy caught talking.'

In 1875 the visitors recommended the appointment of a third master to teach English and writing. Mr Albert West was appointed on a salary of £80 per annum and £15 for lodging and attendance at Church House. He lasted only a few months, having taken 'two of Miss Jackson's boys to Sheringham where they spent

Cartoon of Roberts and staff.

School group c.1897.

the afternoon having tea and supper in one of the inns of the place and returning to Church House at 10 minutes past one on Monday morning.' Mr Charles Brough, third master from 1878 to 1884, left after allegations, largely unsubstantiated, about his 'moral character,' and his two immediate successors emigrated to India and Queensland respectively. The longest-serving third master, William ('Billy') Thorp, was in post between 1888 and 1898, and had 'apparently never heard of discipline or self-discipline, but with whose unruly class nobody attempted to interfere.'

The first known French master, Charles Pichon, was appointed by Elton in the 1860s and left in 1877. Thomas Heywood (1861–1941) described the foreign masters at the school of his day (c.1875) thus: 'Mons. Pichon, the French master, is a jovial soul liked by all. He invites some of us now and then into his house across the way, and makes marvellous fine herb omelettes which we gobble piping hot from the pan. An unwholesome pimple faced German once appeared on the scene for something less than a term. He would stroke the boys furtively and call them his "nice liddle fools". He disappeared suddenly, and was captured on the carrier's van half way to Norwich with his trunk stuffed full of boarders' under-clothing. Socks and shirts recovered, it was thought best to let him continue his flight.' Pichon's successors were generally either French or German Swiss. The last of the French and German masters, Raymond Baudwin (in post 1892–1899), left the school for Heidelberg. Canon Jarvis stated that 'Froggie . . . spent countless hours of misery trying to contend with impossible pupils.'

The number of boarders gradually increased, although given the remoteness of north Norfolk, the general agricultural depression and the poverty of many Norfolk clergymen, their number was never great. By 1864, there were ten. In 1865 Church House, behind the schoolhouse, was purchased and designated as a boarding house. It was run by a dame, Miss Jackson, who lodged the usher, the

Holt Street party to celebrate the wedding of the future King George V and Queen Mary: 1893. The Grammar School dominates the East end of the Market Place.

French master and fifteen boys. The house, although well run, was insanitary and without a good water supply. In 1876 a decline in the number of boarders caused Miss Jackson to abandon the project as uneconomical. She was succeeded by Mr Stephen Bousfield, the second master, and in turn by his successor, Mr Howell. The crisis in sanitation came to a head in June 1886 when one of the boys resident in Church House died of typhoid fever. The house was closed and demolished. Its insanitary condition was aggravated by having been built on part of the churchyard. 'Woodlands', the future boarding house, was considered and rejected as a replacement to Church House. The Governors finally settled on 'Wansbeck House'. The master and second master could, between them, only house about half of those boys needing to board. Some dames determined to undercut their rivals by offering more advantageous terms, and in 1888 we find Miss Withers being told that she must not have as many boarders as heretofore and that 'only one boy can be allowed in a bed.'

In 1880, the school year was changed to three terms, along the lines adopted by most public schools. In 1885 Mr Roberts introduced chemistry into the curriculum and the Governors provided the apparatus and chemicals; the subject was deemed a great success. In the following year, he requested £10 for electrical apparatus to lecture on that and kindred sciences. He delighted pupils with demonstrations of pumps, syphons and preparations of oxygen. Unfortunately, the provision of a laboratory was deemed out of the question and Mr Clement Cozens-Hardy's request for a laboratory and technical education in 1891 and 1892 fell on deaf ears. By 1890 Mr Roberts was urging making classics optional so that the pupils could concentrate on modern languages. In the late 1880s, Mr Roberts introduced shorthand and bookkeeping into the curriculum, which was taught by Mr Willis of Cromer. By 1894, forty-five boys studied shorthand, twelve of whom obtained Pitman's certificates, and eighteen boys were instructed in bookkeeping.

Promising boys were entered for the Cambridge Local Examinations, and from at least 1878 onwards at the annual breaking up, parts of well-known plays and dramatic monologues were performed, including *Le Médecin Malgré Lui*, scenes from *The Rivals*, *Richard III*, *Les Femmes Savantes*, and Mrs Hemans's immortal *Casabianca*. Mr Roberts introduced an annual athletics day in the 1870s for which the Governors provided a horizontal bar, trapeze and five guineas for prizes. The cricket field was continually enlarged and there was a flourishing football club.

The deputation of the Fishmongers in 1890 found Mr Roberts 'worthy of especial commendation' and the examination results were regarded as excellent. In 1895, there were sixteen boys studying Greek; fifty Latin; forty-eight French; three German; twenty-eight mathematics, Euclid (Geometry) and algebra; one trigonometry and high sections; and fifteen physical geography and chemistry. No English literature was taught. The boys were aged 8 to 16 and generally left to enter trade but, between 1858 and 1900, at least twenty-four went to Cambridge, three to Oxford, and one each to Lincoln Theological College and the Universities of London and Edinburgh. Mr Roberts attributed the large numbers leaving school so young to the great depression in agriculture and the lack of exhibitions or scholarships to encourage them to go to university.

Mr Roberts, who had a serious operation in 1896, retired to the Isle of Wight after his last prize day on 27 July 1900. He became the first vicar of Wroxhall, Sandown, where he died on 23 March 1911, aged 77, from the effects of a paralytic stroke. With Roberts's departure, the forty-two year history of the provincial grammar school which provided education for the aspirant middle classes of north Norfolk came to a close.

Acknowledgements for the History prior to 1900

Dr M.J. Crossley Evans would like to thank the following people for their invaluable assistance in compiling the material for the text of the history of the school prior to 1900:

Mr George D. Astley; the late Mr Douglas Baldwin; Mr Michael J. Barrett, FSA; Mrs Janet Bath; Mr R.C.F. Besch; Mrs Jo-Anne Buck; the late Captain W. Bulwer-Long of Heydon Hall; Mr Paul V.A. Colombé; the late Dr A.B. Cottle, FSA, quondam reader in Mediaeval Studies, University of Bristol; Mr Alastair J. Cuthbert; Mr and Mrs Charles R. Daplyn; Miss Hilda M. Davies; the late Mrs A. Bruce Douglas; Mr Eric S. Earl, quondam clerk to the Worshipful Company of Fishmongers; the late Professor Charles S. Elton, FRS; the late Mr Leonard S. Elton; the late Venerable Archdeacon Charles R. Forder; Mr Steven Freeth, keeper of manuscripts at the Guildhall Library, London; Dr Alexander W. Greer; the Revd Stephen S. Gregory; Professor John A. Guy; the late Miss Jane Hales; Professor A. Hassell Smith; the Rt. Hon. the Lord Hastings; Dr Roger L. Highfield, quondam fellow and librarian of Merton College, Oxford; Mrs May Hunter; Miss Jean Kennedy, MBE, and the staff of the Norfolk and Norwich Record Office; Mr Adrian Koh Kok Wee; Mr Kuok Yew Chen; Dr Anthony R. Leech; the master and fellows of Magdalene College, Cambridge; the Revd A. Hugh Mead of St Paul's School; the late Sir Charles Mott-Ratclyffe, D.L.; the late Mr Hugh G. Mullins; Mr Michael O'Brien, quondam clerk to the Worshipful Company of Fishmongers; Mrs Dorothy M. Owen, FSA, quondam keeper of archives at the University of Cambridge; Mrs Nicola H. Press; the late Mr R. John Purdy, CMG, OBE; Mr Paul R. Quarrie, quondam librarian of Eton College; Mr Alan W. Rolfe; the late Dr E. Clive Rouse, MBE, FSA; the late Mr Jack Roy; Mr Michael J. Runnalls; the late Dr R.C. Smail, archivist and fellow of Sidney Sussex College, Cambridge; and Dr Peter J. Wallis of the University of Newcastle upon Tyne; the Librarians of the House of Lords and the House of Commons; the staff of the Bodleian Library, the British Library, and the Public Records Office; the librarians of Gray's Inn, Winchester Cathedral, Westminster School and the City of Portsmouth Record Office; the college archivists of Christ's, Corpus Christi, Gonville and Caius, St John's and Trinity Colleges, Cambridge; and of Balliol and Corpus Christi Colleges, Oxford; the archivist of the University of St Andrew's; the librarians of the Royal Colleges of Physicians and Surgeons; and the staff of the county record offices of Bristol, Cambridgeshire, Cumbria, Essex, Hampshire, Humberside, the Isle of Wight, Leicestershire, Lincolnshire, Northamptonshire, Nottinghamshire and West Sussex.

Selected List of Former Pupils

SIR CHRISTOPHER HEYDON (c. 1571) Astrologer. Wrote *A defense of Judicial Astronomy* 1603.

JAMES HOLMAN (1649) Fellow and later Master of Caius College Cambridge 1700–02.

DR THOMAS GIRDLESTONE (1766) Pioneer of vaccination.

JOHN BURRELL (1769) Early member of the Linnean Society.

SAMUEL FRANK MARRYAT (1830) Travel writer, edited his father's (Captain Frederick Marryat's) posthumous children's book *The Little Savage.*

EDMUND DAWSON ROGERS (1831) First Editor and Founder *Eastern Daily Press.*

WILLIAM RANSOME MESNEY (1848) Missionary in Sarawak. Translated the New Testament into Sea Dyak.

WILLIAM JOSEPH SPRATLING (1854) Pro-Vice Chancellor, University of London.

SIR JOHN HAMMOND (1898) Reader in Agricultural Physiology at Cambridge University. FRS Authority on animal production and animal physiology.

SIR JOHN REITH (1904) First Director General of the BBC 1927–38. Minister of Information and Transport, Works 1940–2. Baron 1940.

SIR WILLIAM HOLMES (1904) Lt. Gen. Command IX Army in the Levant in the Second World War.

DR HEATHCOTE STATHAM (1905) Organist Norwich Cathedral. Conductor Norwich Philharmonic

Society (33 seasons) and London Symphony Orchestra.

SIR CECIL GRAVES (1906) Joint Director General of BBC 1942.

ROBERT MAWDESLEY (1909) Actor. The first Walter Gabriel in *The Archers.*

BEN NICHOLSON (1909) Artist.

JOHN DALY (1912) Bishop of Gambia and the Rio Pongas (at the age of 32), of Accra and of Korea. He lived to celebrate his 50th year as a bishop.

LESLIE EVERETT BAYNES (1912) Aeronautical designer and engineer: early protagonist of the swing-wing principle and designer of flying boats for Short Brothers.

TOM WINTRINGHAM (1912) Commander of the English Battalion, The International Brigade in 1937 at the battle of Jamara in the Spanish Civil War.

SIR TERENCE AIREY (1913) Lt. General GOC Hong Kong. After the War played a major role in reconstruction of Trieste as Military Governor.

SIR ERIC BERTHOUD (1913) HM Ambassador to Denmark and Warsaw.

H. KEMYS BAGNALL-OAKELEY (1914) English sprinter and Long Jump International. Selected for 1928 Olympics.

SIR LENNOX BERKELEY (1914) Composer.

STANLEY LUNT (1914) Three times Amateur Golf Champion and English International.

BRUCE BELFRAGE (1915) Actor and wartime BBC newsreader.

SIR WILLIAM RUSHTON (1915) FRS Physiologist.

PATRICK WADDINGTON (1915) Actor.

DR MOSTYN LEWIS (1916) Long time member of Radio *Brains Trust.*

E. CLIVE ROUSE (1916) Authority on English Mediaeval wall paintings.

SIR PERCY WYN HARRIS (1917) Governor of the Gambia and Everest Mountaineer.

SIR PHILIP TOOSEY (1917) Real-life (and very different!) POW Senior Officer; Bridge on River Kwai.

DICK BAGNALL-OAKELEY (1918) Naturalist, schoolmaster, marksman, artist, photographer, television broadcaster, Norfolk dialect raconteur.

ERSKINE H. CHILDERS (1918) President of Ireland.

CEDRIC BELFAGE (1918) Writer, journalist and KGB agent (according to Mandrake in *The Sunday Telegraph* 1996).

JOHN HAYWARD (1918) Literary scholar, critic, bibliophile, editor, anthologist, biographer, bibliographer.

SIR STEPHEN SPENDER (1918) Writer and poet.

SIR OWEN WANSBOROUGH-JONES (1918) Academic, soldier, civil servant.

SEBASTIAN SHAW (1919) Actor.

BERTRAM STOWELL (1919) England Hockey International.

THE RT REVD JOHN MOORMAN (1919) Bishop of Ripon.

THE RT.HON. SIR BLANSHARD STAMP (1919) Lord Justice of Appeal.

ROBERT MEDLEY (1919) Artist, designer, Royal Academician.

WYSTAN H. AUDEN (1920) Author and poet.

HARRY HODSON (1920) Editor *The Sunday Times,* Fellow of All Souls, Oxford.

JOCELYN SIMON (1920) Lord Simon of Glaisdale, Solicitor General and Lord of Appeal in Ordinary.

SIR JAMES RICHARDS (1921) For 35 years Editor of *Architectural Review*; champion of 'Modernism'.

SIR ROBERT BRAY (1922) General. Deputy Supreme Commander of Allied Command Europe.

JOHN SALTMARSH (1922) Historian. Fellow, Librarian, Archivist and Vice-Provost of King's College, Cambridge.

PAUL WILSON (1922) Mechanical

engineer, Governor of BBC, Labour Life peer (Lord Wilson of High Wray).

DONALD MACLEAN (1923) Spy

JOHN PUDNEY (1923) Author and poet (*For Johnny*).

DAVID KEITH-LUCAS (1924) Aeronautical engineer. Chief Designer for Shorts. Team leader developing Jump Jet.

SIR CHRISTOPHER COCKERELL (1924) Inventor of the Hovercraft.

DAVID LACK (1924) FRS Winner of Darwin Medal. Director of Edward Grey Institute of Field Ornithology at Oxford.

THE RT REVD ROBIN WOODS (1925) Dean of Windsor and Bishop of Worcester.

PETER POOLEY (1926) Founder and first editor of Radio Newsreel (first broadcast 1940).

SIR ALAN HODGKIN (1927) Winner of Nobel Prize for Medicine, President of the Royal Society. Master of Trinity College, Cambridge. Order of Merit.

BENJAMIN BRITTEN (1928) Composer. Baron Britten of Aldeburgh. Order of Merit,

Companion of Honour.

BRIAN SIMON (1928) Professor of Education, University of Leicester.

BORIS FORD (1932) Editor of *Pelican Guide to English Literature*, Professor of Education University of Bristol.

THE RT. REVD DAVID HAND (1932) Anglican Archbishop of Papua New Guinea.

IAN PROCTOR (1932) Yachting designer and journalist. His invention of the Proctor Spar helped to popularise small-boat sailing. His best known design was the Wayfarer.

A.S.M. (MICHAEL) CUMMINGS (1933) Political Cartoonist. Longest-serving contemporary cartoonist at the time of his death drawing for the *Daily Express* for more than 40 years: also *The Sunday Express*, *The Daily Mail*, *Punch* and *Paris Match*.

SIR NIGEL FOULKES (1933) Chairman Civil Aviation Authority.

MICHAEL ALDRIDGE (1933) Actor.

JOHN BRADBURNE (1934) Canonisation candidate; soldier, lay member of Order of St Francis, Warden of the Leper Colony at Mtemwa, Rhodesia (Zimbabwe), seized and murdered by Mugabe's guerrillas in 1979.

ALASTAIR HETHERINGTON (1935) Editor Manchester *Guardian*

DENNIS EAGAN (1937) Bronze medallist Helsinki Olympics. England Hockey. Secretary of Hockey Association.

TOM BOURDILLON (1938) Everest mountaineer 1953; made the assault before Hillary and

Tensing, failing due to breakdown in oxygen apparatus which he had pioneered. Died in an Alpine fall aged 32.

SIR PHILIP DOWSON (1938) Architect. President of Royal Academy of Arts.

PETER BROOK (1939) Theatre Director.

SIR ROBIN IBBS (1939) Chairman Lloyds Bank.

PETER WHITBREAD (1940) Actor.

SIR MARTIN WOOD (1940) FRS Chairman of Oxford Instruments Group. Senior Research Officer, Clarendon Laboratories, Cambridge, into superconductivity and the development of instruments for medical diagnosis.

SIR WILLIAM STUTTAFORD (1942) Founder of Framlington Investment Group.

DR TOM STUTTAFORD (1944) Member of Parliament and Medical Correspondent of *The Times*.

ANDREW MULLIGAN (1945) Irish Rugby International. British Lions.

JOHN TUSA (1945) Broadcaster, Managing Director of BBC World Service, President Wolfson

College, Cambridge, Managing Director of the Barbican Centre.

DR JOHN HAMPTON (1949) Professor of Cardiology, Nottingham University.

STEPHEN FREARS (1954) Film Director.

SIR CHRISTOPHER HOWES (1955) Chief executive of the Crown Estate.

JAMES DYSON (1956) Inventor (bagless vacuum cleaner), businessman.

THE RT REVD PETER LEE (1958) Bishop of Christ the King, Johannesburg.

JOHN LANCHESTER (1972) Prize-winning author.

RICHARD LEMAN (1973) Winner of two Olympic hockey medals: Los Angeles 1984 (bronze) and Seoul 1988 (gold).

JULIAN JARROLD (1974) Film and TV director.

GEORGE STILES (1974) Winner of the Olivier Award for best musical (*Honk!*).

NICK YOUNGS (1976) England Rugby XV.

MATTHEW DICKINSON (1977) Climber of Everest (North Face) 1996. Journalist and TV producer/director.

RODERICK WATKINS (1977) Composer.

Killed in Action

1914–1918

Andrews, E.C.
Armitage, S.W.
Atkin, G.O.H.
Aveling, L.N.
Ayris, N.
Barker, A.S.
Barker, C.N.
Barker, C.W.T.
Barker, H.F.
Barratt, G.R.
Bartleet, H.B.
Batten, J.K.
Beck, J.S.
Beeton, R.H.
Berridge, R.W.
Biden, L.T.G.V.
Bird, A.C.
Blackburne, E.
Booth, B.B.
Brownsword, D.A.
Busk, H.A.
Carnegie, D.A.
Chapman, H.E.
Chestney, F.W.
Cobon, H.G.
Cole, A.H.
Cornish, B.G.
Crick, C.G.
Crosse, E.C.M.
Crosse, M.E.B.
Cunnell, D.C.
Davies, L.F.St J.
Drey, A.
Duff Gordon, C.L.
Dulley, D.C.C.
Dye, G.H.
Ellis, J.C.
Elwell, E.E.
Estcourt, A.C.
Evans, P.H.
Fenchelle, G.J.
Foster, J.M.
Fox, C.E.
Frost, G.K.
Giles, G.E.
Gissing, W.I.
Goodall, G.M.L.
Graves, A.H.
Halsey, F.W.
Harvey Jones, F.M.
Hawksley, G.
Herron, A.R.
Hill, C.A.
Hill, M.C.

Holland, A.L.
Hooper, P.J.
Hyde, A.N.
Inglis, R.
Jacques, D.W.
Jarvis, A.B.
Johnson, G.B.
Kempson, J.R.
Kirch, C.
Knowles, H.
Malcolm, A.A.
Marriott, S.G.
Mobbs, E.S.
Neal, A.B.
Newsum, C.N.
Nicholson, J.A.
Palmer, H.S.
Partridge, R.H.
Phillimore, J.P.
Preston, S.
Prideaux Brune, E.N.
Proctor, J.N.W.A.
Richardson, D.B.
Robinson, H.H.K.
Rogers, D.S.
Rumsby, R.W.
Russell, H.B.
Scott Holmes, H.F.
Shaw, C.F.
Sheppard, C.A.
Sillem, T.G.
Simpson, J.H.
Smith, V.N. (Staff)
Soman, L.A.
Spurrell, F.J.D.
Thicknesse, R.S.
Thorn, H.
Trendell, M.H.W.
Tyler, G.C.
Vallancy, H.H.D.
Walker, F.C.
Warwick, J.D.B.
Wells, C.D.
White, E.G.
Wills, A.L.
Wilson, I.M.
Wright, J.M.S.

1939–1945

Andrews, R.H.
Anthony, D.N.W.L.
Arnott, J.W.
Arnott, P.
Askew, G.D.
Atherton, J.L.
Barham, R.F.
Bartlett, G.T.
Beach Thomas, M.
Bell, P.H.
Beney, D.L.
Birch, A.M.A.
Blackburn, G.
Blunden, K.O.
Borradaile, J.W.
Borrow, G.H.
Bristow, R.W.
Bull, S.
Chaple, E.A.H.
Clause, P.W.A.
Cross, G.S.
Daly, R.O.
Diver, J.
Dodds, R.D.
Dollar, G.
Eachus, G.T.
Foster, C.L.
Game, D.
Gibbs, J.A.
Gregson, M.G.
Griffith, T.P.L.
Gros, E.L.
Hall, H.N.T.
Hamilton, G.C.
Hawksley, R.G.
Hayden, G.G.
Hicks, A.D.S.
Hinde, E.J.F.
Holt, G.W.
Howard, E.B.
Humphrey, W.C.L.
Huslop, E.J.
Kennedy, J.McL.
Kerridge, O.L.
King, G.S.
Lakeman, M.W.
Langley, J.R.
Leach, P.A.
Levitgt, J.R.
Lindsell, E.S.
Lowe, J.J.
Mace, H.G.
Maclean, I.
Martin, E.J.B.

Mayor, S.R.
McAnally, J.
McCuaig, D.K.
McCuaig, E.N.
Mocok, R.C.
Morris, G.
Mosseri, L.N.
Newsum, G.H.
Nichols, F.P.R.
Norgate, R. Le G.
Norman, O.D.
Pears, J.H.
Powell, R.H.
Reynolds, B.F.
Reynolds, O.B.
Roberts, P.A.S.
Robertson, S. D.G.
Roger Smith, B.H.
Round, J.H.B.
Sadler, M.T.C.
Scott, J.P.E.
Scott, R.B.
Sharp, A.C.
Shaw, J.
Simon, M.H.H.
Soddy, J.R.
Spender, M.A.
Stilwell, N.T.
Story, G.F.E.
Stuart, A.H.E.
Stuart, G.C.E.
Swainson, C.C.
Tetley, W.A.
Thompson, D.W.
Tomson, T.F.
Toosey, A.D.
Trench, J.P.
Trobridge, D.A.G.
Wathes, P.J.L.
Webb, D.M.
Westley, G.N.
Whiteley, M.J.
Whittome, J.E.G.
Wilkinson, D.W.
Willcock, A.J.
Williams, J.R.
Winn, K.L.
Womersley, F.G.
Wood, C.B.
Wood, T.B.
Woodwark, P.A.
Wooldridge, J.A.
Zillessen, W.H.

Masters of Holt Grammar School 1562–1900

— Robinson	there 1571
— Harrison	there 1574
Unnamed	*c.*1580
Christopher Williams	*c.*1584–1602
The Revd Richard Snoden	1602–1605
The Revd Francis Catlyn	1605–1606
Thomas Tallis	1606–1639 and 1640
The Revd Nethanial Gill	1639–1640
Thomas (later Sir Thomas) Witherley	1640–1644
John Fenn	1644–1646
The Revd Francis Wright	1646–1659
The Revd William Hicks	1659–1660
The Revd Henry Mazy	1660–1665
The Revd John Goodman	Acting Master 1665–1667
The Revd Thomas Bainbridge	1667–1692
The Revd William Reynolds	1692–1716
The Revd David Duncombe (or Duncan)	1716–1729
John Holmes	1729–1760
John Knox	1760
James Smith	1760–1787
Thomas Atkins	1787–1806, 1807–1809
The Revd Mr Babington	Acting Master 1806–1807
The Revd Benjamin Pullan (later Pulleyne)	1809–1857
The Revd Charles Allen Elton,	1858–1867
Unnamed	Acting Master 1865–1866
William Henry Hooper (later the Revd)	Acting Master 1866–1867
The Revd Reginald Jolliffe Roberts	1867–1900

Ushers and Second Masters 1562–1900

Nicholas Stephenson	1602–1606
The Revd John Watson	–1621
The Revd Thomas Cooper	1627–1632
Nicholas Davie	1632–1638
The Revd Thomas Cooper	1638 (did not take up office)
Henry Luce	1638–1639
No usher	1639–1640
Henry Luce	1640
Timothy Cutler	1640/1–1643
The Revd Thomas Cooper	1643–1644
No usher	1645
Henry Mazy	1658–1660
The Revd John Goodman	1661–1665
Thomas Kellway	*c.*1689–1692
William Chambers	1692
Thomas Garrett	1692–1695
William Rowland	1695
Thomas Turner	1696–1697
Thomas Plumstead	1697–1704

John Reynolds	1705–1708
John Fox	1708
William Selth	1708–1713
John Spurling	1713–1714
William Chaplyn	1714–1715
John Brooke	*c.*1718
John Holmes	*c.*1725
Edward Read	1729
No usher	*c.*1751–1759
Christopher Stangroom	*c.*1770
David Kinnebrook	*c.*1796–*c.*1801
The Revd Robert Davies	1810–1811
Peter Barney	1811–1813
Daniel Carr	1813–1821
James Sturley	1821
The Revd Thomas Beckwith	1821–1828
The Revd William Robert Taylor	1828–1843
John Slann*	1843–1851
William Allen Rudkin	1851
John Hubbert Kent	1851–1857
J. Rodney Phillips	1858–1860
Berney Wodehouse Raven	1860
Charles Frederick Furbank	1860–1862
Frederick Roy Dowson	1862–1863
George W. Antiss	1863–1864
Henry David Jones	1864–1865
William Henry Hooper	1865–1866
Matthew Walter Tunnicliff	1866–1867
William Remington Backhouse	1867
John Robinson Wells	1867
Robert Stokes	1867–1869
Robert Campbell Conolly	1869–1871
John Lowndes	1871–1872
Stephen Bousfield	1872–1880
John Henry Howell	1881–1900

* first recorded Second Master.

Headmasters of Gresham's School 1900–2001

George W.S. Howson	1900–1919
J. Ronald Eccles	1919–1935
Joseph H. Foster	Acting Headmaster 1935
Philip S. Newell	1935–1944
A. Bruce Douglas	Acting Headmaster 1944
Martin J. Olivier	1944–1955
A. Bruce Douglas	Acting Headmaster 1955
Logie Bruce Lockhart	1955–1982
Timothy P. Woods	1982–1985
John K. Coleridge	Acting Headmaster 1985
Hugh R. Wright	1985–1991
John H. Arkell	1991–2002
Antony Clark	2002–

Second Masters and Deputy Heads 1900–2002

John Goodrich Wemyss Woods	1900–1907
James Ronald Eccles	1907–1919
John Chambré Miller	1919–1928
Joseph Foster	1928–1942
Bruce Douglas	1942–1963
Bernard Sankey	1963–1970
Paul Colombé	1970–1977
John Coleridge	1977–1985
Richard Copas	1985–2001
Susan Smart**.	2001–

**first Deputy Head.

Headmasters of the Junior School

John Williams	1954–1969
Michael Hughes	1969–1979
Neville Jones	1979–1984

Headmasters of the Preparatory School

Tony Cuff	1984–

Heads of the Pre-Preparatory School

Penny Moore	1984–1991
Lesley Gillick	1991–1997
Daphne Dawson-Smith	1997–2002
Janette Davidson	2002–

Index for Chapters 1–6

Index for Chapter 7